アメリカ英語日常会話辞典

南雲堂

はしがき

　日本人の英語熱は世界一である。これは1998年のTOEICテストにはっきり反映され，受験者総数約280万人のうち日本人が6割以上の約180万人を占めた。ところが実力は990点満点中，約4割しか取れていない。TOEFLの成績になると更に悪く世界でビリに近い163番目である（1997年）。
　TOEIC，TOEFLテストを実施しているアメリカの非営利教育機関が上記の年数以後データを公表していないが，年を追うごとにますます日本人の両テストの成績は悪化していると巷間言われている。
　日本人の英語熱と実力との乖離の原因はいくつかあるが，ここでは特に下記の2点を取り挙げたい。

第I　辞典には誤りが多すぎる

　あるべき姿の辞典が市場にないことも非常に大きな原因である。辞典の不備が英語をわざわざ難しくして学習者はその犠牲者になっていることを筆者のアメリカ留学時代の苦い経験上断言したい。
　筆者は高校生のとき単語は一語の単語で覚えても意味はなく，辞典の中に出ている例文の中で覚えるべきだと英語の先生に強く勧められた。以来辞書を引くといつも必ず各単語の例文を算数の九九と同様，すらすら口について出てくるまで各文を何度も朗読した。辞書の執筆陣は一流大学の高名な教授たちだったので全幅の信頼を置いていた。誤りがあるとは微塵も考えなかった。ところが，後にアメリカ留学し，レポートを提出したところ全く使われていないJapanese Englishや，ある小説家の独特な表現の例文をたくさん覚え込んでいることを教授たちに指摘された。筆者はこのとき味わった挫折感，失望は長年経った今でも，つい先日のことのようにはっきりと覚えている。まさに地面にたたきつけられた，言葉では言い尽くせない苦い，苦い，苦い経験であった。
　問題なのは筆者が初めて留学してから何十年も経っている。この間，日本の社会は非常に大きく大きく変わった。特に1990年代に入ってからは，明治維新，敗戦に次ぐ3番目の大転換期にあると言える。終身雇用をはじめとする多くの社会の制度，また今まで肯定視されてきたありとあらゆる価値観，やり方が大きく見直されてい

る大激動期にある。しかしながら，こと英語の辞典，特に和英辞典には旧態依然である。いや旧態依然どころか更に悪化していると言っても過言ではない。そこに出ている表現は「新和英辞典」「新英和辞典」と「新しい……」というタイトル名で売り出されているにもかかわらず，19世紀，20世紀の初頭までしか使われていない表現を満載しているからである。更に悪いことには英米の区別を明示していないで並記しているのも利用者に不親切である。筆者はこういう辞典を見る度に隔靴掻痒を覚えるどころか，執筆者の学問に対する横柄さに驚きを禁じえない。執筆者はこの不適切な辞典がどれほど利用者を惑わしているかを強く心にとどめるべきである。

辞典が次々に改訂されたにもかかわらず以前より悪化したと前述したのは執筆陣にネイティブスピーカーの名前を以前と違って大きく出しているからである。これはネイティブがその辞典の中の全文に目を通している印象を読者に与える。しかし筆者はネイティブは参加していないと断言したい。それはネイティブが参加していたらありえない誤りが多すぎるからである。人間のやることには誤りは多少つきまとうであろう。しかし筆者が声を大にして言いたいことは明らかな誤りが多すぎ，利用者を犠牲者にしていることである。執筆者の謙虚さを強く促したい。例を若干紹介しよう。どの辞典（和英のみならず，英和辞典）にも共通する誤りの例をいくつか挙げてみよう。

1 時刻を尋ねられて「ちょうど5時です」と言うとき，It's just 5:00.と出ている。しかし「ちょうど5時です」に相当する英語は It's exactly 5:00.である。詳細は本辞典の25ページを参照されたい。

また買物して支払うときレジの人が「ちょうど200ドルです」と述べる場合は $200 even.で Just $200.は使われていない。詳細は155ページを参照されたい。

just が「ちょうど」の意味で使われるのは次のように時刻とか金額などの数字が出てこないときである。

That's just what I was going to say.
（それはちょうど私が言おうとしていたことです）

2 「アパート」を辞典で調べると an apartment house が出ているが1970年頃から使われていない。詳細は本辞典126ページを参照されたい。

3 one-room apartment が某和英辞典に出ているが，これは Japanese English, 英語では studio apartment と言う。詳細は本辞典126ページを参照されたい。

4 2DK のアパートに 2-room apartment を紹介しているが使われていない。英語では寝室として使っていなくとも bedroom を使い two-bedroom apartment と言う。

5「心配している」に be anxious about を be worried about とイコールであるかのように紹介しているが両者は同意語ではない。be anxious about は結果などを「心配している」というときに使われている。従って be worried about はいつも等しくない。I was so anxious about the test results that I had a sleepless night.（私はテストの結果が非常に心配だったので夜，寝られなかったんです）詳細は本辞典45ページを参照されたい。

6「太っている」＝be fat と辞典に出ているが be fat は「でぶ」という意味。詳細は本辞典82ページを参照されたい。

7「浮気をする」に betray を出しているが betray は男女間のではなく一般的な意味での「裏切る」，日本語では夫婦間の「浮気する」にも妻に「裏切られた」という日本語につられて betray を紹介しているが誤り。詳細は本辞典115ページを参照されたい。

第2 辞典は現代英語を紹介していない

どの辞典を調べても出ていない表現が多数ある。若干具体例を紹介しよう。

1「彼は接待が上手」と述べるとき He's a good host. が非常によく使われているが紹介している辞典がない。詳細は本辞典54ページを参照されたい。

2「フランス大使館はこの先です」は日常の会話によく出てくるがどの辞典にも出ていない。英語では次のように言う。The French Embassy's down [up] the street.（フランス大使館はこの先です）詳細は本辞典158ページを参照されたい。

3「安くする」＝give a good price がよく使われているが紹介している辞典がない。Can you give me a better price on that car?
（あの車をもっと安くしてくれますか）

詳細は本辞典154ページを参照されたい。

4「安い」＝cheap と覚えている人が多いであろう。これも使われているが「安い」＝good deal ［buy］　This is a good deal ［buy］.（これは安いよ）を紹介している辞典がない。詳細は本辞典153ページを参照されたい。

5「色が合う」を辞典で調べると使われていない mix ［harmonize］ well with が出ている。よく使われている work with は紹介されていない。That green jacket works well with your black skirt.（そのグリーンの上着はあなたの黒のスカートに合っています）詳細は本辞典96ページを参照されたい。

6「振られる」を辞書で調べると jilt が出ているが，今は dump を使うのにこの語は全く紹介されていない。
Nancy dumped Steve.（ナンシーはスティーヴを振ったんです）詳細は本辞典111ページを参照されたい。

　筆者はアメリカに初めて留学して，辞典に夥しい数の誤りがあり，これが英語を必要以上に難しくしていることを知った。以来誤りのない辞典を書き，筆者が味わった挫折感を利用者に味あわせない辞典を書くことが筆者の使命のように思え，長年研鑽してきた。この努力の成果により，あるべき姿の辞典を出版できることになり非常に安堵している。この辞典は利用者に必要以上に英語を難しくしていることから解放し，ひいては日本人の TOEIC, TOEFL の得点力がアップし，日本人全体の英語力向上に大きく貢献するだけでなく，今後出版される英語の辞典にも大きな一石を投ずることになると筆者は強く確信している。
　筆者はすでに第2弾を出す用意もできている。ぜひ読者の皆さんのご感想をお聞かせ願いたい。
　この歴史に残る画期的な辞典を出版するに際して南雲堂の南雲一範社長にいろいろご理解を賜り，筆者の執筆意欲を駆り立てて下さったことに対してここで深く感謝申し上げたい。また青木泰祐編集部長には編集面のみならず，その他いろいろとお世話になり心からお礼を申し上げたい。
　最後にボストンアカデミーの福原正子教務部長にも本辞典誕生にいろいろな面で精魂を傾けてくれたことをここで深く感謝申し上げたい。

この辞典の特色について

世界標準語に認知
されたアメリカ英語

　アメリカ英語とイギリス英語は一般に考えられている以上に表現上の差がある。本辞典はアメリカ英語日常会話辞典というタイトル名が示している通りアメリカ英語を紹介している。多くの辞典はイギリスでしか使われていないのに、その明記なしにアメリカ英語と並記していることは利用者を惑わせている。筆者はイギリス英語は無視せよと言うつもりはないが、日本人にとって外国語である英語を2種類同時に覚えようとすること自体に無理があると断言したい。アメリカ人はイギリス英語を知らない。またイギリス人もアメリカ英語を知らない。英語を必要以上に難しくしている理由のひとつは辞典がアメリカ英語とイギリス英語の2種類を説明なしに並記して紹介しているところもあることを強く指摘したい。従って今後の辞典はアメリカ英語辞典、イギリス英語辞典と別々にすべきである。

　1980年頃から、ビジネスの世界は国境がなくなり始めた。1999年代にインターネットが世界的に普及され始めると共に、ビジネスの世界のボーダレス化は更に加速化された。インターネットはアメリカが開発したものなので、世界の諸民族を結ぶ言葉は英語、それもイギリス英語ではなく、アメリカ英語を話せることが過去数年前から全世界的に当然視され始めている。過日の英字紙によると以前イギリス英語を学習してきたヨーロッパの人たちも今はアメリカ英語を学習している。

　インターネットは今後ますます普及するので、アメリカ英語がますます重要視されるであろう。

　以上の理由で日本人はイギリスとビジネスやその他で特別な関係がない限りアメリカ英語に集中して学習することが適切と筆者は考えている。もしイギリス英語も同時に学習すべきと言うのなら、オーストラリア英語、アイルランド英語も同時に学習する必要性が出てくることになる。

インフォーマント

使用頻度は，別記の米国人インフォーマントから取ったアンケート調査結果に基づいている。見解が割れるときは同一項目について50名以上にアンケートを取り，世代による差もあるのでインフォーマントは30〜45歳に限り，全員大卒以上で，南部以外の出身者である。

従来の辞典では正しい英語か否かを問題にしているが，本辞典では実際にどの位広く使われているかという観点から調査した結果を示した。それは正しくなくとも現在広く使われていることは将来正しい英語として確立していくからである。例を挙げればアメリカ人は slowly, quickly, well（上手にの意味で）の代りに slow, quick, good のほうをずっとよく使っているからである。
He speaks English good.（彼は英語を上手に話す）

◎インフォーマント・リスト

Amy Bruni	Andrew Hoge	Ann Hodgkin
Barbara Canover	Barbara Meller	Brian Nelson
Carol Russel	Carolina Harrison	Catherline Edwards
Cathy Adams	Charles Hoffman	Chris Sanders
Christiana Spengler	Cindy O'connor	David Eckholm
Deborah Tyler	Douglas Rhode	Elizabeth Eliot
Frank Harrison	Gerald Gorman	Gregory Kirk
Howard Broad	Jane Dao	Janice Adams
Jean Norris	Jeffrey Russel	Julia Bernstein
Leslie Dale	Lisa Merluzzi	Maria Brooke
Mary Kirkpatrick	Mike Kurz	Nancy Maloy
Nina Bergstein	Norman Alfven	Patricia Milikan
Paul Weber	Richard Fisher	Rose Anderson
Sally Tilton	Sarah Malone	Sarah Wines
Stephen Carter	Susan Cohen	Susan Venable
Thomas Altman	Tom Sanger	Victoria Kinzer
Wiliam Fox	William Smith	

合計50名のインフォーマントの協力を得た。全員アメリカの南部を除く大学卒の米国人。

◎インフォーマントの利用と選択の仕方

インフォーマントの利用に際して次の4点を頭に置く必要がある。

1 アメリカの学者は口語英語のインフォーマントとしては不適切

　アメリカ人の学者は一般の人よりすぐれた意見を持っていると考えがちである。しかし日常会話的な表現になると筆者の経験では不適切である。彼らは堅い文章,文学で使う表現や,すたれた表現を日常使うからである。これはアメリカ人のみならず日本人にも同じことが言えると思う。

2 日本語が流暢なアメリカ人はインフォーマントとしては不適切

　日本語に流暢なアメリカ人は日本人的な英語を話すはっきりした傾向があるからである。このことは日本人で英語が上手な人は英語的な日本語を話すことからもうなずけるであろう。

3 日本在住年数が長いアメリカ人はインフォーマントとしては不適切

　日本の在住年数が長いということはアメリカを長く不在していることである。日本語も英語も時代と共に使われる頻度に大きな変化が出てくる単語がある。また全く使われなくなったり,逆に新しく使われ始める語が多数ある。これらは俗語とは限らない。社会状勢の変化によって新しく使われる語がどんどん出てくる。これらの流れは無視できない。

4 若年層（25歳以前）と熟年層（55歳以上）はインフォーマントには不適切

　若年層は避けた。筆者の経験上彼らは英語をよく知らないからである。このことは日本人の若年層の日本語を考えれば納得がいくであろう。筆者の経験では「言質」という表現を知っている日本人の若者（大卒を含めて）は極めて少ない。

　熟年層（55歳以上）の人たちは30〜40年前にはよく使われていたが,現在あまり使われていない表現を使う大きな傾向がある。一例を挙げれば現在60歳以上の女性は little woman（妻）と呼ばれると喜ぶが若い女性は怒る。

　日本人はアメリカ人なら誰でも現在使われている英語を話すと思っているように思える。しかしインフォーマントをただ参加させても生きた英語の慣用の事実を引き出せない。彼らの力を十分に引き出すには利用する日本人の側にも文章英語だけ

でなく，話す英語にも深く精通している能力が要求される。従って彼らが分からないときは知ったかぶりをされないで I'm not sure. と言わせるだけの英語力が利用する側にあって，初めて正しい英語の慣用を引き出せることを強く指摘したい。アメリカ人を参加させながら誤りが多い辞典や本が多いのはこの点に原因がある。

構成・使用頻度表示

　本辞典では各見出しの類語を数種類挙げ，それらすべてに使用頻度をつけている。既刊の辞典では皆無である。この点も本辞典の一大特色である。

　各章の中の見出しは状況の流れに応じて構成している。(a)(b)…で語義区分を行ない，必要により下位区分として●，次の区分として1) 2)…を使用。

　（　）印で示した日本語の例文に対する英訳例をⒶⒷⒸ…で掲げ，アメリカ英語における実際の使用頻度を次の記号で表示した。

　　☆　　1番よく使われる　　　　　△　　ときどき使われる
　　◎　　非常によく使われる　　　　▽　　まれに使われる
　　○　　よく使われる　　　　　　　×　　使われない

　例文中の［　］内は交換可能，（　）内は省略可能であることを示す。

卑語などについて

　性に関係する語句を用いた表現，呪いの表現，一部の敬虔なクリスチャンが抵抗を示す神を冒瀆する表現なども必要に応じて収録した。これらは従来の辞典では十分な記述がないことが多かったが，本辞典では使用頻度の高いものはきちんと紹介した。これを知らないとコミュニケーションに支障をきたすからである。多くの場合，注をつけて注意を喚起した。

省略形

　本辞典では，話し言葉で用いられる表現については，be 動詞，have，助動詞などの省略形を用いて表記した。

　例：This suit's off-the-rack. (is →'s)　　Obesity'll kill you. (will →'ll)

　通常は主語が人称代名詞でないときはこうした省略形では書かないが，本辞典では話し言葉の実際の姿を紹介するために省略形を用いている。

本辞典の内容の一部または全部の無断転載は著作権法違反になります。転載される場合は，南雲堂あて許諾申請をお願いいたします。

目　次

はしがき　iii

この辞典の特色について　vii

第1章　あいさつ・ちょっとした一言・呼びかけの表現 …………1
第2章　元気に関する表現 …………………………………………15
第3章　時間に関する表現 …………………………………………25
第4章　感情・気持に関する表現 …………………………………33
第5章　性質に関する表現 …………………………………………53
第6章　人間関係に関する表現 ……………………………………60
第7章　容姿に関する表現 …………………………………………78
第8章　服装に関する表現 …………………………………………94
第9章　男女間に関する表現 ………………………………………108
第10章　暮らし・住居に関する表現 ………………………………120
第11章　レストラン・ホテルでの表現 ……………………………134
第12章　食事・料理に関する表現 …………………………………142
第13章　買物に関する表現 …………………………………………153
第14章　道順に関する表現 …………………………………………157
第15章　交通機関に関する表現 ……………………………………163
第16章　健康・病気に関する表現 …………………………………172

INDEX　192

第1章
あいさつ・ちょっとした一言・呼びかけの表現

1 「あいさつ」
(a) 朝のあいさつ
　　（お早うございます）
　　◎ Ⓐ Good morning!
　　（お早う）
　　◎ Ⓑ Morning!
　　◎ Ⓒ G'morning!
　　◎ Ⓓ Hi!
　　◎ Ⓔ Hi there!
　　◎ Ⓕ Hello!
　　［注意］(1) 文尾に名前を添えるとよりいい感じを与える。
　　(2) ⒶⒷⒸは日本語の「お早う」と違って午前中，つまり11時59分59秒まで使える。
　　(3) 辞典にⒹⒺは日本語の「おす」に当たると出ているが次の理由で等しくない。
　　　日本語の「おす」は男性同士で対等の立場でしか使われていないのに対して，ⒹⒺは親しみを込めてあいさつするときは男性のみならず女性の間，また上司に対しても使われている。

(b) 午後のあいさつ
　　（今日は）
　　◎ Ⓐ Good afternoon!
　　◎ Ⓑ Hi!
　　◎ Ⓒ Hi there!

◎ Ⓓ Hello!
　　［注意］(1) G'morning!, Morning! は使われているが G'afternoon!,
　　　　Afternoon! は使われていない。
　　(2) ⒷⒸはくだけたあいさつ表現。

(c) **夜のあいさつ**
　　（今晩は）
　　◎ Ⓐ Good evening!
　　◎ Ⓑ Hi!
　　◎ Ⓒ Hi there!
　　◎ Ⓓ Hello!
　　［注意］G'morning!, Morning! は使われているが G'evening!, Evening! は使われていない。

(d) **別れるとき**
　　● 朝・昼・夜
　　（さようなら，ジム）
　　◎ Ⓐ Good-bye, Jim.
　　◎ Ⓑ So long, Jim.
　　◎ Ⓒ Bye, Jim.
　　◎ Ⓓ Bye-bye, Jim.
　　［注意］Ⓐは誰にでも使える。ⒷⒸⒹはくだけた表現。

　　● 午後
　　（楽しい1日をお過ごし下さい）
　　☆ Ⓐ Have a nice day.
　　◎ Ⓑ Have a good day.
　　◎ Ⓒ Enjoy the rest of the day.
　　◎ Ⓓ Good day.
　　◯ Ⓔ Enjoy the day.
　　［注意］ⒸⒺのように enjoy を使うと少し改まった響きになる。

　　● 午後5時以降
　　（楽しい夜をお過ごし下さい）
　　◎ Ⓐ Have a nice evening.
　　◎ Ⓑ Have a good night.
　　◎ Ⓒ Good night.

第 1 章　あいさつ・ちょっとした一言・呼びかけの表現

△ ⓓ Enjoy the evening.

(e) 思いがけなく知人・友人に出会ったとき
(リンダ：お会いできてうれしいわ)
☆ Ⓐ Good to see you (again).
☆ Ⓑ Nice to see you (again).
◎ Ⓒ It's good to see you.
◎ Ⓓ It's nice to see you.

(f) 思いがけない場所で知人・友人に会ったとき
(ここであなたにお会いするとは思いませんでした)
◎ Ⓐ This is the last place I'd ever have expected to see [meet] you.
◎ Ⓑ This is the last place I'd ever expect to see [meet] you.
○ Ⓒ Fancy meeting you here.
○ Ⓓ Fancy seeing you here.

(g) 意味なく相手の健康を尋ねるとき
(お元気ですか)
◎ Ⓐ How're you?
◎ Ⓑ How're you doing?
◎ Ⓒ How you doing?
◎ Ⓓ How's it going?
○ Ⓔ How're things?
○ Ⓕ How're things going?
△ Ⓖ How's the world treating you?
[注意] 多くの日本の辞典・教材に知人の健康を尋ねるときに使われていると出ているが実際，初めて会う人に「今日は」の意味でもよく使われている。ⒷⒸもⒶと同様
(元気です)
☆ Ⓐ Fine.
☆ Ⓑ All right.
☆ Ⓒ OK.
☆ Ⓓ Great.
◎ Ⓔ I'm fine.
◎ Ⓕ I'm all right.
◎ Ⓖ I'm OK.
◎ Ⓗ I'm great.

- ○ Ⓘ No complaints.

2 「じゃまたね」
(じゃまたね)
- ☆ Ⓐ See you later.
- ☆ Ⓑ See you.
- ◎ Ⓒ See you around.
- ◎ Ⓓ Talk to you.
- ○ Ⓔ Talk to you later.
- ○ Ⓕ See you soon.
- ○ Ⓖ I'll see you later [around].
- ○ Ⓗ I'll see you.
- △ Ⓘ I'll see you soon.

3 「久し振りです」
(a) 昔の部下・学生・友人に会って
(久し振りだね)
- ◎ Ⓐ Long time no see.
- ◎ Ⓑ Where've you been hiding yourself?
- ◎ Ⓒ Where've you been keeping yourself?

(b) 昔の上司・恩師などに会って
(お久し振りです)
- ◎ Ⓐ It's been a long time!
- ◎ Ⓑ It's been (quite) a while!
- ◎ Ⓒ It's been ages!
- ◎ Ⓓ I haven't seen you in ages [in a long time].
- ◎ Ⓔ Haven't seen you in ages.

(c) 女性が男性の友人に，または女性の友人に会って
(お久し振りね)
- ◎ Ⓐ I almost [nearly] forgot what you looked like.
- ◎ Ⓑ It's been forever.
- ◎ Ⓒ Long time no see.
- ◎ Ⓓ Where've you been hiding [keeping] yourself?

4 「すみません」

(a) 謝罪する内容に言及しない場合
(本当にすみません)
☆ Ⓐ I'm very sorry.
◎ Ⓑ I feel very sorry.
○ Ⓒ I'm terribly [really] sorry.
○ Ⓓ I feel terribly [really] sorry.
○ Ⓔ I really feel sorry.
[注意] 謝ることで弁償することが発生してくる交通事故のようなときは、たとえ話し手は自分に落ち度があったことを認めていてもⒶ～Ⓔを使わない点が日本語と違う。アメリカ人はこのような場面で相手の非をできるだけ多く並べ立てる。

(b) 今現在相手に迷惑をかけている内容に言及して謝罪する場合
(お邪魔してすみません)
I'm sorry ☆ Ⓐ to bother you.
　　　　　 ◎ Ⓑ for bothering you.
　　　　　 ○ Ⓒ I'm bothering you.

(c) 迷惑の内容が現在完了の継続内容の場合
(こんなに長くお待たせしてしまってすみません)
I'm sorry ☆ Ⓐ I've kept you waiting this long.
　　　　　 ◎ Ⓑ to have kept ...
　　　　　 ○ Ⓒ for having kept ...

5 「(詫びに対して) どういたしまして」

(a) **I'm so sorry.** と深く謝罪されたとき
(どういたしまして)
☆ Ⓐ That's [It's] OK [all right].
◎ Ⓑ Don't mention it.
◎ Ⓒ Don't worry about it.
○ Ⓓ It was [It's] nothing.
△ Ⓔ That was [That's] nothing.
△ Ⓕ Don't be worried about it.

(b) **Excuse me.** と軽く詫びられたとき
(どういたしまして)
◎ Ⓐ That's OK [all right].

◎ Ⓑ No problem.
○ Ⓒ Don't worry about it.

6 「(感謝されて) どういたしまして」
(a) 高級な店で客が礼を言ったとき
(どういたしまして)
◎ Ⓐ It's my pleasure.
◎ Ⓑ My pleasure.
◎ Ⓒ You're welcome.
○ Ⓓ Certainly.

(b) コンビニ・スーパーなどで客が礼を言ったとき
(どういたしまして)
◎ Ⓐ You're welcome.
◎ Ⓑ Don't mention it.
◎ Ⓒ Sure thing.
◎ Ⓓ You bet.
○ Ⓔ Sure.
○ Ⓕ You betcher [betcha].
△ Ⓖ My pleasure.
△ Ⓗ It's my pleasure.

(c) 友人・家族同士などで丁重さが求められていないとき
(どういたしまして)
◎ Ⓐ You're welcome.
○ Ⓑ Don't mention it.
○ Ⓒ Sure (thing).
△ Ⓓ You bet [betcha].

7 「何とおっしゃったのですか」
(a) 丁重に尋ねる場合
(何とおっしゃいましたか)
◎ Ⓐ I beg your pardon?
◎ Ⓑ Beg your pardon?
◎ Ⓒ Pardon me?
◎ Ⓓ I'm sorry?
◎ Ⓔ Excuse me?

第1章　あいさつ・ちょっとした一言・呼びかけの表現

　　◎ Ⓕ Would you repeat that ［it］ please?
　　［注意］Ⓐが1番丁重な響きがある。その他はほぼ同じ。

(b)　普通に尋ねる場合
　　（何て言いましたか）
　　◎ Ⓐ Pardon?
　　◎ Ⓑ Sorry?
　　◎ Ⓒ Can you say that again?
　　◎ Ⓓ Can you come again?
　　◎ Ⓔ Come again?
　　◎ Ⓕ What did you say?
　　◎ Ⓖ What's that?
　　◎ Ⓗ What?

(c)　乱暴に尋ねる場合
　　（何だって）
　　◎ Ⓐ What's that?
　　◎ Ⓑ What?
　　［注意］ⒶⒷとも強い語調で発音する。

8 「紹介する」

(a)　個人に対して紹介する場合
　　●顔を合わせて紹介する場合
　　1) 親しげに紹介するとき
　　（スティーブ，友人のウィリアム・スミスを紹介するよ）
　　Steve, ☆ Ⓐ I want you to meet my friend, William Smith.
　　　　　　◎ Ⓑ meet my friend, William Smith.
　　　　　　◎ Ⓒ I'd like you to meet my friend, William Smith.
　　　　　　○ Ⓓ let me introduce my friend, William Smith to you.
　　　　　　△ Ⓔ let me introduce to you my friend, William Smith.
　　2) かしこまって紹介するとき
　　（スティーヴ，私の友人のウィリアム・スミスをご紹介します）
　　Steve, ◎ Ⓐ allow me to present to you, my friend, William Smith.
　　　　　　◎ Ⓑ let me present to you, my friend, William Smith.
　　　　　　○ Ⓒ allow me to present my friend, William Smith.
　　　　　　○ Ⓓ let me present my friend, William Smith.
　　●顔を合わせて紹介することと，名前や電話番号を教えるだけのいずれにも取

れる場合
(すてきな男性をご紹介しますよ)
I'll ◎ Ⓐ fix you up with a nice guy.
　　 ◎ Ⓑ set you up with a nice guy.
　　 ◎ Ⓒ introduce you to a nice guy.
［注意］ⒶⒷⒸいずれも男女間のみならず，弁護士，会計士などのビジネス上の紹介にも非常によく使われている。

(b) 大勢の人に対して紹介する場合
(皆さん，フロリダ州知事をご紹介します)
Ladies and gentlemen, ◎ Ⓐ I give you the governor of Florida.
　　　　　　　　　　 ◎ Ⓑ let me introduce [present] to you the governor of Florida.
　　　　　　　　　　 ◎ Ⓒ allow me to present to you the governor of Florida.
［注意］Ⓒは非常に改まった響きがある。かしこまった表現を使う人の間ではよく使われている。

9 「会う」

(a) 知り合うとき
(お会いできて嬉しいです)
☆ Ⓐ Nice to meet you.
◎ Ⓑ It's nice [I'm glad] to meet you.

(b) 知り合うプロセスがあるとき
(どこで奥さんと知り合ったのですか)
Where did you ◎ Ⓐ get to know your wife?
　　　　　　　 ◯ Ⓑ meet to know your wife?

(c) 約束して友人，知人，ビジネス上の人と会うとき
(私は今日の午後私の弁護士と会います)
I'm going to ◎ Ⓐ see [meet] my lawyer this afternoon.
　　　　　　 ◯ Ⓑ meet with my lawyer this afternoon.

(d) 約束して場所を明示して会うとき
(エセックスホテルで会いましょう)
Let's ◎ Ⓐ meet at the Essex Hotel.

　　　　○ Ⓑ see each other at the Essex Hotel.
　　　　× Ⓒ see at the Essex Hotel.

(e) **会う日時，曜日を明示するとき**
　　（近いうちに会いましょう）
　　Let's ◎ Ⓐ meet ［get together］ one of these days.
　　　　　○ Ⓑ see each other one of these days.

(f) **偶然会うとき**
　　（私は駅へ行く途中でビルに会いました）
　　◎ Ⓐ I met ［saw, ran into, bumped into, happened to see, happened to meet］ Bill on the way to the station.
　　◎ Ⓑ I met Bill by chance on the way to the station.

10 「知り合う」

(a) **初めて紹介された場合**
　●改まった口調で述べるとき
　（お知り合いになれてとてもうれしく思っています）
　I'm ◎ Ⓐ very pleased to meet you.
　　　　○ Ⓑ delighted ...
　　　　× Ⓒ very delighted ...
　［注意］(1) be delighted には very の意味が入っている。従ってⒸは使われていない。
　(2) ⒷのほうがⒶより改まった響きがある。

　●普通の口調で述べるとき
　（お知り合いになれてとてもうれしいです）
　◎ Ⓐ I'm really ［very］ glad to meet you.
　◎ Ⓑ It's really ［very］ nice to meet you.
　○ Ⓒ I'm really glad to (get to) know you.
　○ Ⓓ It's really nice to (get to) know you.
　［注意］ⒸⒹの get to know you は男性同士の間ではよく使われているが，女性から男性にはそれほど使われていない。

　●くだけた調子で述べるとき
　（お知り合いになれてうれしいです）
　◎ Ⓐ Nice ［Glad, Happy］ to meet you.

○ Ⓑ Nice to get to know you.

(b) パーティーなどの退出時に「お知り合いになれてよかった」と述べる場合
　●普通に述べるとき
　（お知り合いになれてよかったです）
　☆ Ⓐ It was nice meeting [to meet] you.
　◎ Ⓑ Nice meeting [to meet] you.
　○ Ⓒ It was nice getting [to get] to know you.
　△ Ⓓ I was glad to meet you.
　△ Ⓔ I was glad to get to know you.

　●強調して述べるとき
　（お知り合いになれてとてもよかったです）
　◎ Ⓐ It was really good meeting [to meet] you.
　◎ Ⓑ It was really good to get to know you.
　○ Ⓒ Really good meeting [to meet] you.
　△ Ⓓ It was really good getting to know you.

　●改まった口調で述べるとき
　（お知り合いになれてよかったです）
　△ Ⓐ It was nice getting [to get] acquainted with you.
　△ Ⓑ I was pleased [glad] to meet you.

11 「本当ですね」
(a) 改まった話し方をする必要がないとき
　（リンダ：すごく寒いわね）
　Linda: It's really cold.
　（ジェーン：本当ね）
　Jane: ☆ Ⓐ Oh, yeah.
　　　　☆ Ⓑ That's right.
　　　　☆ Ⓒ It sure is.
　　　　☆ Ⓓ You're right.
　　　　◎ Ⓔ You said it.
　　　　◎ Ⓕ You can say that again.
　　　　◎ Ⓖ You're telling me.
　　　　◎ Ⓗ I'll say.
　　　　◎ Ⓘ You bet.

◎ ⓙ You got [have] that right.
[注意] Ⓐ～ⓙまで天気に限らず相づちをうつとき広く使える。

(b) 改まった話し方をする必要があるとき
〈高級レストランなどで〉
(客：今日はすごく寒いですね)
Customer: It's really cold today.
(ウエイター：本当ですね)
Waiter: ◎ Ⓐ Yes, it certainly is.
　　　　 ◎ Ⓑ I'll say.
　　　　 ◎ Ⓒ Yes, it is.
　　　　 △ Ⓓ Yes, indeed.

12 「残念です」
(リンダ：高い熱があってパーティーに行けないのよ)
Linda: I have a high fever, so I can't come to the party.
(ナンシー：それは非常に残念だね)
Nancy: ☆ Ⓐ I'm really sorry to hear that.
　　　　◎ Ⓑ That's too bad.
　　　　◎ Ⓒ That's really disappointing.
　　　　◎ Ⓓ What a big disappointment!
　　　　○ Ⓔ That really sucks.
　　　　○ Ⓕ That's a real shame.
　　　　○ Ⓖ That's a real bummer [drag].
[注意] Ⓔは30歳以下年代が下がるにつれて使用頻度は上がる。

13 「(約束を破ったり，遅刻ばかりする人に対して責める気持で) どうしたんだい」
(どうしたんだい)
What's ☆ Ⓐ your problem?
　　　　◎ Ⓑ the problem with you?
　　　　◎ Ⓒ wrong with you?
　　　　◎ Ⓓ the matter with you?
　　　　○ Ⓔ come over you?
[注意] ⒶⒷⒸⒹⒺいずれも相手が顔色が悪い人に対して同情的に尋ねるときにも多少使われる。どちらであるかは口調による。

14 「すごい」
(夫：宝くじで1等が当ったよ)
Husband: I won the lottery!
(妻：すごい)
Wife: ☆ Ⓐ That's great!
　　　◎ Ⓑ Great!
　　　◎ Ⓒ Terrific!
　　　◎ Ⓓ Amazing!
　　　◎ Ⓔ Awesome!
　　　◎ Ⓕ Incredible!
　　　◎ Ⓖ Super!
　　　◎ Ⓗ Unbelievable!
　　　◎ Ⓘ Fantastic!
［注意］辞典に Swell!, Peachy!, Capital! が出ているが使われていない。

15 「くどい」
(スティーヴ：約束の日に必ずお金を返してくれよ)
Steve: Don't forget to pay the money back on time.
(ディヴィッド：くどいぞ)
David: ◎ Ⓐ I heard this (all) before.
　　　 ◎ Ⓑ I heard this already.
　　　 ○ Ⓒ You've already said that.
　　　 × Ⓓ You're repeating.
［注意］Ⓓが辞典に出ているが使われていない。

16 「呼びかけ」
(a) **女性に呼びかける場合**
　●40〜50歳の人が20〜25歳の女性に，または50歳以上の人が40歳前の女性に
(通行人：もしもし，鍵を落しましたよ)
Passerby: ☆ Ⓐ Excuse me, Miss, you dropped your key.
　　　　　☆ Ⓑ Hey, Miss, ...
　　　　　◎ Ⓒ Miss, ...
　　　　　○ Ⓓ Hello, ...
　　　　　○ Ⓔ Hello, Miss, ...
　　　　　△ Ⓕ Hi, Miss, ...
　　　　　△ Ⓖ Hi there Miss, ...
［注意］Miss は既婚，未婚を問わず使われている。相手の女性が若く見える

[12]

第1章　あいさつ・ちょっとした一言・呼びかけの表現

という気持ちを持って話し手である男（女）性が呼びかけるとき使われている。

●25歳以上の女性の店員に
(高級デパートでの客：もしもし，お願いできますか)
Customer at an expensive department store:
◎ Ⓐ Excuse me, Ma'am, can you help me?
◎ Ⓑ Ma'am, ...
◎ Ⓒ Hello, ...
[注意]　既婚，未婚に関係なく使われている。

●45歳以上のお客が18才位以上の女性の店員に，または55歳以上のお客が30歳位の女性の店員に
(高級デパートでの客：もしもし，お願いできますか)
Customer at an expensive department store:
☆ Ⓐ Excuse me, young lady, can you help me?
☆ Ⓑ Young lady, ...
◎ Ⓒ Hello, ...

●5歳位の女の子に
(レストランでの客：お嬢ちゃま，ナプキンを落しましたよ)
Customer at a restaurant:
☆ Ⓐ Excuse me, little girl, you dropped your napkin.
☆ Ⓑ Little girl, ...
◎ Ⓒ Hey, ...
◎ Ⓓ Hello, ...
△ Ⓔ Hi, ...
[注意]　ⒸⒹⒺには「お嬢ちゃま」という意味はない。

(b) 男性に呼びかける場合
●20歳以上の人が12歳以下の男の子に，または60歳以上の人が35歳以下の男性に
(通行人：すみません，新聞を落しましたよ)
Passerby:　☆ Ⓐ Excuse me, young man, you dropped your paper.
　　　　　☆ Ⓑ Hey, young man, ...
　　　　　◎ Ⓒ Young man, ...
　　　　　○ Ⓓ Hello, ...
　　　　　○ Ⓔ Hello, young man, ...

△ Ⓕ Hi, young man, ...
　　　△ Ⓖ Hi there, ...

● お客が20歳以上の男性の店員に
（高級デパートでの客：もしもし，お願いできますか）
Customer at an expensive department store:
◎ Ⓐ Excuse me sir, can you help me?
◎ Ⓑ Sir, ...
◎ Ⓒ Hello, ...

● 5歳位の男の子に
（レストランでの客：お坊っちゃま，ナプキンを落しましたよ）
Customer at a restaurant:
☆ Ⓐ Excuse me, little boy, you dropped your napkin.
☆ Ⓑ Little boy, ...
◎ Ⓒ Hey, ...
◎ Ⓓ Hello, ...
△ Ⓔ Hi, ...

● ねえあなた
（ねえあなた，あなたの留守中淋しかったわ）
I missed you while you were gone, ◎ Ⓐ sweetheart.
　　　　　　　　　　　　　　　　　◎ Ⓑ honey.
　　　　　　　　　　　　　　　　　◎ Ⓒ dear.
　　　　　　　　　　　　　　　　　○ Ⓓ daring.
　　　　　　　　　　　　　　　　　△ Ⓔ my dear.

[注意] (1) Ⓐは年令に関係なく広く使われている。ⒷⒸは30歳以上の人の間で，Ⓓは45歳以上の人の間で広く使われている。Ⓔは60歳以上の人の間で使われている。
(2) Ⓐ〜Ⓔは文頭でも等しくよく使われている。
(3) Ⓐ〜Ⓔいずれも男性から女性へ，また女性から男性に対しても使われる性別により使用頻度に差はない。
(4) ⒶⒷⒸⒹⒺいずれも小文字のほうが大文字で書くより普通。

第2章 天気に関する表現

1「いいお天気です」
(いいお天気ですね)
☆ Ⓐ Beautiful day, isn't it?
☆ Ⓑ Nice day, isn't it?
☆ Ⓒ Beautiful weather, isn't it?
◎ Ⓓ Good weather, isn't it?
◎ Ⓔ Lovely day [weather], isn't it?
[注意] (1) 文頭に It's を付けると使用頻度は◎の普通になる。
(2) いいお天気＝It's fine. と思っている人が多いが，アメリカでは全く使われていない。

2「いやな天気」
(いやな天気ですね)
It's ☆ Ⓐ bad weather, isn't it?
　　　 ◎ Ⓑ nasty weather, ... ?
　　　 ◎ Ⓒ awful weather, ... ?
　　　 ◎ Ⓓ terrible weather, ... ?
　　　 △ Ⓔ ugly weather, ... ?
[注意] 辞典に inclement, foul, wretched が出ているが会話ではまれにしか使われていない。

3「晴れ上がる」
(明日までには晴れ上がるでしょう)
☆ Ⓐ The sun'll be out by tomorrow.

☆ Ⓑ The weather'll clear up by ...
◎ Ⓒ It'll clear up by ...
◎ Ⓓ The weather'll be sunny by ...
◎ Ⓔ It'll be sunny by ...
◎ Ⓕ We'll have nice weather by ...
◯ Ⓖ The sun'll come out by ...
◯ Ⓗ The sky'll be sunny by ...

4 「晴れのち曇り」
(明日は晴れのち曇りでしょう)
☆ Ⓐ Tomorrow's weather'll be fair to cloudy.
☆ Ⓑ The weather tomorrow'll be fair to cloudy.
◎ Ⓒ It'll be fair to cloudy tomorrow.

5 「久し振りにいい天気」
(今日は久し振りにいい天気です)
Today we have nice weather for the first time in
◎ Ⓐ ages.
◎ Ⓑ a long time.
◎ Ⓒ many days.
◎ Ⓓ several days.
△ Ⓔ a long while.
［注意］天気の悪かった期間としてはⒶが1番長く，ⒷⒸⒺⒹの順で短くなる。

6 「暑くなる」
(明日は暑くなるでしょう)
It'll ☆ Ⓐ be hot tomorrow.
　　　◎ Ⓑ get hot ...
　　　◯ Ⓒ become hot ...

7 「蒸し暑い」
(日本の夏は蒸し暑いんです)
Summer in Japan's ☆ Ⓐ muggy.
　　　　　　　　　◎ Ⓑ sticky.
　　　　　　　　　◎ Ⓒ hot and humid.
　　　　　　　　　◯ Ⓓ steaming hot.
　　　　　　　　　◯ Ⓔ sweltering.

第 2 章　天気に関する表現

　　　　○ Ⓕ like an oven.
　　　　△ Ⓖ steaming [steamy].

8「暑くてやりきれない」
　（暑くてやりきれませんね）
　☆ Ⓐ I can't stand this heat.
　◎ Ⓑ I can't deal with this heat.
　◎ Ⓒ I can't handle this heat.
　○ Ⓓ I can't put up with this heat.
　○ Ⓔ I can't bear this heat.
　○ Ⓕ The heat's unbearable.
　△ Ⓖ The heat's intolerable.
　［注意］辞典に The heat's insupportable. が出ているが使われていない。

9「焼けつくように暑い」
　（外は焼けつくように暑いですね）
　It's ☆ Ⓐ unbelievably hot outside.
　　　☆ Ⓑ incredibly hot ...
　　　◎ Ⓒ like an oven ...
　　　◎ Ⓓ as hot as hell ...
　　　○ Ⓔ sizzling [scorching, a scorcher, burning hot, scorching heat, broiling] ...
　　　○ Ⓕ so hot you could fly an egg on the sidewalk ...
　　　△ Ⓖ boiling hot ...
　［注意］辞典に It's baking hot. が出ているが使われていない。

10「うだるように暑い」
　（うだるように暑いです）
　It's ☆ Ⓐ really hot and humid.
　　　☆ Ⓑ very hot and humid.
　　　☆ Ⓒ like a sauna.
　　　◎ Ⓓ terribly [awfully] hot and humid.
　　　○ Ⓔ really like an oven.
　　　○ Ⓕ stifling hot.
　［注意］辞典に boiling hot が「うだるように暑い」の表現として紹介されているが，この表現には humid のニュアンスはない。従って「焼けつくように暑い」の和訳に等しい。

11 「(天候が) 続く」

(a) **through [until]** がある場合
(この暖かい天気は週末一杯続くと私は思います)
I hope this warm weather'll ☆ Ⓐ last through the weekend.
　　　　　　　　　　　　　◎ Ⓑ continue ...
　　　　　　　　　　　　　○ Ⓒ stay ...
　　　　　　　　　　　　　△ Ⓓ keep ...

(b) **for**＋期間がある場合
(この涼しい陽気は数日間続くでしょう)
This cool weather'll ☆ Ⓐ last [continue] for a few days.
　　　　　　　　　　◎ Ⓑ stay on [go on] ...
　　　　　　　　　　○ Ⓒ keep going ...
　　　　　　　　　　△ Ⓓ keep [carry on, hold] ...

(c) 非人称の **It** を主語にとるある種の動詞を従える場合
(火曜日まで雨が降り続くでしょう)
It'll ☆ Ⓐ continue to rain until Tuesday.
　　　☆ Ⓑ continue raining ...
　　　◎ Ⓒ keep (on) raining ...
　　　○ Ⓓ go on raining ...

[注意] 同様の文型をとる動詞は snow (雪), sleet (みぞれ), sprinkle (霧雨) など。

12 「空模様からすると」

(空模様からするとまもなく雨が降るでしょう)
☆ Ⓐ From the way the sky looks, it looks like it's going to rain soon.
◎ Ⓑ Judging by the look of the sky, it ...
◎ Ⓒ From the look of the sky, it ...

13 「天候に関係なく」

(私は天気に関係なく明日あなたの事務所に行きます)
I'll come to your office tomorrow ☆ Ⓐ whether it rains or not.
　　　　　　　　　　　　　　　　☆ Ⓑ even if it rains.
　　　　　　　　　　　　　　　　◎ Ⓒ rain or shine.

　　　　　　　　　　　○ Ⓓ regardless of the weather.
　　　　　　　　　　　△ Ⓔ no matter the weather.
［注意］辞典に in fair weather or foul, in all weather(s) が出ているが前者はまれ，後者は使われていない。

14 「(天気が) すぐ変わる」
（この頃は天気がすぐ変わりますね）
These days the weather ◎ Ⓐ changes a lot.
　　　　　　　　　　　◎ Ⓑ changes fast.
　　　　　　　　　　　◎ Ⓒ is always changing.
　　　　　　　　　　　◎ Ⓓ changes frequently.
　　　　　　　　　　　○ Ⓔ is changeable.
　　　　　　　　　　　○ Ⓕ changes quick.

15 「変わりやすい天気」
（変わりやすい天気ですね）
It's ☆ Ⓐ strange weather, isn't it?
　　　◎ Ⓑ odd weather, ...?
　　　○ Ⓒ changeable weather, ...?
［注意］辞典に fickle, unsettled が出ているが使われてもまれ。

16 「崩れる」
（この暖かい天候は数日後に崩れます）
This warm ☆ Ⓐ weather'll end in a few days.
　　　　　◎ Ⓑ weather won't last until a few days.
　　　　　○ Ⓒ weather won't stay until a few days.
　　　　　△ Ⓓ weather won't hold until a few days.
　　　　　× Ⓔ weather won't break until a few days.
［注意］Ⓔが辞典に出ているが使われていない。但し「悪天候がよくなる」の意味から次のように使われている。This bad weather'll break soon.（この悪天候はまもなくよくなるでしょう）

17 「寒いです」
(a) **普通に述べるとき**
（寒いですね）
　☆ Ⓐ Cold, isn't it?
　◎ Ⓑ It's cold, isn't it?

◎ Ⓒ Cold enough for you?

(b) **強調するとき**
(すごく寒いですね)
It's ☆ Ⓐ really cold, isn't it?
　　◎ Ⓑ very cold, isn't it?
　　◎ Ⓒ freezing cold, isn't it?
　　◎ Ⓓ damn cold, isn't it?
　　◎ Ⓔ fucking cold, isn't it?
　　○ Ⓕ biting cold, isn't it?
　　○ Ⓖ icy cold, isn't it?
［注意］Ⓔは非常によく使われているが性表現なので自分から使うことは勧めない。

18 「…になりそうです」
(土砂降りになりそうです)
☆ Ⓐ It looks like it's going to rain really hard.
◎ Ⓑ It looks like we're going to have a lot of rain.
◎ Ⓒ It looks like we're going to get a lot of rain.
◎ Ⓓ It looks like as if it's going to rain really hard.
◎ Ⓔ It looks like we're in for downpour.
◎ Ⓕ It looks like it's going to downpour.
◎ Ⓖ Looks like it's going to rain really hard.
○ Ⓗ Looks like a lot of rain.

19 「土砂降り」
(今朝から雨が土砂降りです)
☆ Ⓐ It's been really pouring [coming down] since this morning.
☆ Ⓑ It's been raining really [really raining] hard since …
◎ Ⓒ It's been raining very hard since …
◎ Ⓓ The rain's been really coming down since …
◎ Ⓔ The rain's been really falling [falling really] hard since …
○ Ⓕ It's been really raining [raining really] fast [heavy] since …
○ Ⓖ It's been raining cats and dogs since …
○ Ⓗ It's been really raining in buckets since …
○ Ⓘ It's been coming down in buckets since …
○ Ⓙ The rain's been falling very hard [in buckets] since …

第2章　天気に関する表現

20 「小雨が降る」
(小雨が降っています)
☆ Ⓐ It's drizzling.
◎ Ⓑ It's raining a little.
○ Ⓒ It's raining lightly.

21 「霧がかかる」
(今晩は非常に深い霧がかかるでしょう)
☆ Ⓐ It'll be really foggy this evening.
◎ Ⓑ We're going to have (a) really heavy fog ...
◎ Ⓒ We're going to get (a) really heavy fog ...
◎ Ⓓ There'll be really heavy fog ...
◎ Ⓔ It'll get really foggy ...
○ Ⓕ There'll be really thick fog ...
○ Ⓖ There'll be really dense fog ...
○ Ⓗ It'll become really foggy ...
△ Ⓘ It'll really fog up this evening.

22 「霧が深い」
(今朝は霧が深かった)
☆ Ⓐ It was really foggy this morning.
◎ Ⓑ It was very foggy ...
◎ Ⓒ There was a heavy fog ...
◎ Ⓓ There was a thick fog ...
○ Ⓔ There was a dense fog ...

23 「霧が晴れる」
(霧は正午までには晴れるでしょう)
The fog'll ☆ Ⓐ clear up by noon.
　　　　　 ◎ Ⓑ lift by noon.
　　　　　 ○ Ⓒ clear by noon.
［注意］辞典に clear away が出ているが使われていない。

24 「にわか雨にあう」
(私は今日仕事からの帰り道でにわか雨にあったんです)
I got [was] caught ☆ Ⓐ in the rain on my way home from work.

　　　　　　　○ Ⓑ in the shower ...
　　　　　　　○ Ⓒ in the shower rain ...
［注意］(1) ⒶⒷⒸの the は a も等しく使われている。どちらを使うかはすでに言及されて特定されているか否かで使い分ける。
(2) 辞典に be overtaken by a shower が出ているが使われていない。

25 「激しい雷雨」
（私は今日仕事からの帰り道でものすごい激しい雷雨にあったんです）
I was [got] caught in a really ☆ Ⓐ bad thunderstorm
　　　　　　　　　　　　　　　◎ Ⓑ terrible ...
　　　　　　　　　　　　　　　◎ Ⓒ awful ...
　　　　　　　　　　　　　　　○ Ⓓ heavy ...
　　　　　　　　　　　　　　　○ Ⓔ severe ...
on my way home from work.

26 「…年振りの大雨」
（これは10年振りの大雨です）
This is the heaviest ☆ Ⓐ rain in ten years.
　　　　　　　　　　◎ Ⓑ rain we've had in ...
　　　　　　　　　　○ Ⓒ rainfall in ...
　　　　　　　　　　○ Ⓓ rainfall we've had in ...
［注意］「10年振りの大雪」は rain を snow, snowfall に，「10年振りの嵐」は rain を storm にすれば表現できる。使用頻度は雨と同じ。

27 「雨がやむ」
（雨がやんだよ）
◎ Ⓐ It's stopped raining.
◎ Ⓑ The rain's stopped.
◎ Ⓒ The rain's died down.
◎ Ⓓ The rain's let up.
［注意］辞典に left off, died が出ているが使われていない。

28 「雪がたくさん降る」
（雪がたくさん降っているよ）
☆ Ⓐ It's snowing really hard.
☆ Ⓑ It's really snowing hard.
◎ Ⓒ The snow's really coming down.

○ Ⓓ The snow's falling.
　△ Ⓔ It's snowing heavy [fast].
　[注意] 辞典に The snow's falling thick and fast. The snow's coming down hard. が出ているが使われていない。

29 「吹雪です」
　(吹雪だよ)
　It's ☆ Ⓐ a blizzard.
　　　　◎ Ⓑ a snowstorm.
　[注意] 辞典に The snow's raging. が出ているがまれ。

30 「ひどい吹雪」
　(ひどい吹雪だよ)
　It's a ☆ Ⓐ really bad snowstorm.
　　　　☆ Ⓑ really bad blizzard.
　　　　◎ Ⓒ really awful blizzard [snowstorm].
　　　　◎ Ⓓ really terrible blizzard [snowstorm].
　　　　○ Ⓔ really horrible blizzard [snowstorm].
　　　　○ Ⓕ really driving snowstorm.
　　　　○ Ⓖ severe blizzard [snowstorm].
　　　　○ Ⓗ whiteout.
　[注意] Ⓗが1番ひどい吹雪のニュアンスがある。ⒷとⒼの severe blizzard が2番。blizzard のほうが snowstorm より強い響きはあるが混用もされている。

31 「風がごうごう吹く」
　(昨夜は風がごうごう吹いていました)
　The wind was ☆ Ⓐ really blowing last night.
　　　　　　　☆ Ⓑ blowing really hard ...
　　　　　　　☆ Ⓒ howling ...
　　　　　　　◎ Ⓓ blowing like crazy ...
　　　　　　　○ Ⓔ roaring ...
　[注意] Ⓓが1番強く吹いていたニュアンスがある。

32 「風が出てくる」
　(風が出てきました)
　☆ Ⓐ It's getting windy.

◎ Ⓑ The wind's getting strong.
◎ Ⓒ It's becoming windy.
○ Ⓓ The wind's growing.
○ Ⓔ The wind's rising.
[注意] 辞典に The wind's blowing up ［coming up, springing up］. が出ているが使われていない。

33 「風がひゅうひゅう吹いています」
(外は風がひゅうひゅう吹いています)
◎ Ⓐ The wind's whistling outside.
△ Ⓑ It's whistling outside.
[注意] The wind's moaning ［blowing with a whistle］. が辞典に出ているが使われていない。

34 「風が強い」
(今日は風が強いですね)
◎ Ⓐ It's windy today.
○ Ⓑ There's a strong wind today.
○ Ⓒ It's blowing hard today.

35 「風がやむ」
(風が明け方頃やみました)
The wind ☆ Ⓐ died down towards dawn.
　　　　　◎ Ⓑ let up ...
　　　　　○ Ⓒ stopped blowing ...
[注意] (1) 辞典に The wind died away ［fell, went down］. It's stopped blowing. が出ているが使われていない。
(2) die down, let up は共に「風がなぐ」の意味であったが今は「風がやむ」の意味で使われている。

第3章 時間に関する表現

1 「何時」
(a) 漠然と尋ねるとき
　　（何時ですか）
　　☆ Ⓐ Can you tell me the time?
　　◎ Ⓑ What time is it?
　　◎ Ⓒ What time do you have?
　　◎ Ⓓ Do you have the time?
　　○ Ⓔ What's the time?

(b) あなたの時計でと明示するとき
　　（あなたの時計では何時ですか）
　　☆ Ⓐ Do you have the right time?
　　☆ Ⓑ Can you tell me the right time?
　　◎ Ⓒ Do you have the correct time?
　　◎ Ⓓ Can you tell me the correct time?
　　○ Ⓔ What time does your watch say?
　　○ Ⓕ What time is it by your watch?

2 「ちょうど」
　　（ちょうど7時です）
　　☆ Ⓐ Exactly 7:00.
　　◎ Ⓑ It's exactly 7:00.
　　◎ Ⓒ 7:00 on the dot [nose].

○ Ⓓ 7:00 exactly.
[注意] (1) どの辞典にも「ちょうど」＝just が出ているが「ちょうど」の意味では全く使われていない。「まだ7時です」の意味ならよく使われている。
(2) just が「ちょうど」の意味で使われるのは次のような時間，数字がないときである。
That was just what I was going to say.
(それは私がちょうど言おうとしていたことです)

2 「(到着の時間がスケジュール通りの意味での）ちょうど…」
(彼らの飛行機はちょうど10時に着きました)
Their plane arrived ◎ Ⓐ at 10:00 as scheduled.
　　　　　　　　　◎ Ⓑ on time at 10:00

3 「まだ」
(a) 時間がたつのが早いと思ったとき
(まだ9時だよ)
It's ◎ Ⓐ just 9:00.
　　 ◎ Ⓑ only 9:00.
[注意] 辞典に just＝「ちょうど」と出ているが just＋時間のときはこの意味はない。just が時間以外の内容を従えたときは just＝「ちょうど」になる。

(b) 時間がたつのが遅いと思ったとき
(まだ9時です)
◎ It's still 9:00

4 「(時間を) 合わせる」
(a) 一般的に述べるとき
(私の時計は今朝テレビの時間に合わせたから合っていますよ)
My watch's right because ◎ Ⓐ I set my watch by the TV signal.
　　　　　　　　　　　　 ◎ Ⓑ I adjusted my watch ...

(b) 進んでいた（遅れていた）ので合わせたと述べるとき
(あの時計は進んでいます。合わせて下さい)
That clock's fast. ◎ Ⓐ Fix it.
　　　　　　　　　○ Ⓑ Adjust it.
　　　　　　　　　○ Ⓒ Set it right.
　　　　　　　　　△ Ⓓ Set it correct.

第3章　時間に関する表現

(c) 「（目覚ましを何時に）合わせる」と述べるとき
　　（目覚ましを6時に合わせて下さい）
　　Set the alarm clock ☆ Ⓐ for 6:00
　　　　　　　　　　　　◎ Ⓑ to go off at 6:00.

5 「進む」
（私の時計は1日5分進むんです）
My watch ☆ Ⓐ gains five minutes a day.
　　　　　◎ Ⓑ runs five minutes fast a day.
　　　　　○ Ⓒ runs fast by five minutes a day.

6 「遅れる」
（私の時計は1日5分遅れるんです）
My watch ☆ Ⓐ loses five minutes a day.
　　　　　◎ Ⓑ runs five minutes slow a day.
　　　　　○ Ⓒ runs slow by five minutes a day.

7 「（時計が）進んでいる」
(a) 「…分進んでいる」と述べる場合
　　（あの時計は5分進んでいます）
　　That clock's five minutes ☆ Ⓐ fast.
　　　　　　　　　　　　　　　◎ Ⓑ ahead.
　　　　　　　　　　　　　　　○ Ⓒ early.

(b) 「何分進んでいる」と述べる場合
　　（あの時計は何分進んでいるのですか）
　　◎ Ⓐ How fast's that clock?
　　◎ Ⓑ How many minutes fast's that clock?
　　○ Ⓒ How many minutes ahead's that clock?

8 「（遅れている時計を）進める」
（あの時計を10分進めて下さい）
　☆ Ⓐ Please set that clock ten minutes fast.
　◎ Ⓑ Please set that clock ten minutes ahead.
　○ Ⓒ Please put that clock ten minutes fast.
　○ Ⓓ Please put that clock ten minutes ahead.

△ Ⓔ Please advance that clock ten minutes.

9 「急ぐ」
(b) **目的地に言及する場合**
（私は急いで市役所へ行かなければならないんです）
I have to ◎ Ⓐ rush ［run, fly, hurry］ to city hall.
　　　　　○ Ⓑ dash to ...
　　　　　△ Ⓒ make a dash to ...
　　　　　× Ⓓ hurry up to ...
［注意］Ⓓの hurry up to は命令文以外では使われていない。

(b) **命令文の場合**
（急いで下さい）
Please ☆ Ⓐ hurry up.
　　　　◎ Ⓑ hurry.
　　　　△ Ⓒ rush.
　　　　△ Ⓓ be quick.
　　　　△ Ⓔ speed it up.
▽ Ⓕ make haste.

(c) **急いで何かを持ってこさせる場合**
（急いで私の計算機を持ってきて）
☆ Ⓐ Hurry. Bring my calculator.
◎ Ⓑ Bring my calculator quick.
○ Ⓒ Hurry and bring my calculator.
○ Ⓓ Hurry up. Bring my calculator.

10 「急いで帰る」
（私たちは急いで事務所へ帰らなければならないんです）
We've got to ◎ Ⓐ fly back to the office.
　　　　　　○ Ⓑ race back ...
　　　　　　○ Ⓒ dash back ...
　　　　　　○ Ⓓ rush back ...
　　　　　　○ Ⓔ hurry back ...
［注意］Ⓐが1番急いでいるニュアンスがあり、ⒷⒸⒹⒺの順で下がる。

11 「(車のスピードを) 急ぐ」

(a) 普通に述べる場合
 (急いで下さい)
 ☆ Ⓐ Step on it, please.
 ◎ Ⓑ Step on the gas, please.
 ◎ Ⓒ Drive [Go] faster, please.
 ○ Ⓓ Speed (it) up, please.
 ○ Ⓔ Get a move on, please.
 ○ Ⓕ Give it some gas, please.

(b) 強く述べる場合
 (急いでよ)
 ◎ Ⓐ Gun it.
 ○ Ⓑ Put the pedal to the metal.
 △ Ⓒ Give it a lot of gas.

12 「急いでいません」
(私たちはこれを急いでいません)
 ◎ Ⓐ We can wait for this.
 ◎ Ⓑ There's no hurry [rush] ...
 ◎ Ⓒ We're not in a rush ...
 ○ Ⓓ We're not in a hurry ...
 △ Ⓔ We're not pressed ...

13 「急いで連れて行く」
(彼らはひどいけがをしています。急いで彼らを病院へ連れて行こう)
They're badly hurt. Let's ◎ Ⓐ rush them to the hospital.
　　　　　　　　　　　　　◎ Ⓑ race ...
　　　　　　　　　　　　　◎ Ⓒ bring ...
　　　　　　　　　　　　　◎ Ⓓ get ...
　　　　　　　　　　　　　◎ Ⓔ take them to the hospital immediate-
　　　　　　　　　　　　　　　ly [right away, quickly, quick].
　　　　　　　　　　　　　× Ⓕ dash them to the hospital.

[注意] (1) Ⓕが辞典に出ているが使われていない。
(2) Ⓐ〜Ⓓには「すぐに」の意味が入っているが，Ⓔの take には入っていないので immediately, right away, quickly, quick が必要である。
(3) Ⓐ〜Ⓓにも immediately, right away, quickly, quick を付けて強調してもよく使われている。

[29]

(4) Ⓓの get には「すぐ連れて行く」の意味を紹介している辞典はないが，実際にはよく使われている。

14 「(交通機関に) 間に合う」
((電話で) あなたは 7 時の飛行機に間に合ったの)
Did you ☆ Ⓐ catch the 7:00 flight?
　　　　◎ Ⓑ get on the 7:00 flight?
　　　　◎ Ⓒ make (it to) the 7:00 flight?
　　　　◎ Ⓓ get to the 7:00 flight on [in] time?
　　　　◎ Ⓔ get to the airport on [in] time for the 7:00 flight?
　　　　○ Ⓕ make it on the 7:00 flight?
　　　　○ Ⓖ get to the airport for the 7:00 flight on [in] time?
　　　　△ Ⓗ arrive at the airport for the 7:00 flight on [in] time?
　　　　△ Ⓘ arrive in [on] time for the 7:00 flight?

15 「(約束に) 間に合う」
(あなたは約束に間に合ったの)
☆ Ⓐ Did you make it to the appointment?
◎ Ⓑ Did you make the appointment?
◎ Ⓒ Were you on [in] time for the appointment?
◎ Ⓓ Did you get to the appointment on [in] time?
△ Ⓔ Did you make it for the appointment?

16 「遅れる」
(a) **コンサート・会合などのように動かないものに**
●最初の部分に遅れたとき
(私たちはコンサートに遅れてしまったんです)
We ◎ Ⓐ were late for the concert.
　　◎ Ⓑ didn't get to the concert on time.
　　◎ Ⓒ didn't make (it to) the concert.
　　◎ Ⓓ weren't on time for the concert.
　　◎ Ⓔ didn't get to the hall in [on] time for the concert.
　　○ Ⓕ didn't get to the concert in time.
　　○ Ⓖ didn't make it for the concert.
　　△ Ⓗ weren't in time for the concert.
［注意］Ⓕはコンサートの始めから終りまで見そこなったという場合と，最初の部分だけ遅れてしまった場合の両方に等しくよく使われているが，Ⓗの型は

第3章　時間に関する表現

コンサートの最初の部分という一部に間に合わなかっただけでなく，主として始めから終わりまで見そこなったときには非常によく使われている。

●全く見ることが（または出席）できなかったとき
（私たちはコンサートに遅れてしまったんです）
We ◎ Ⓐ missed the concert.
　　 ◎ Ⓑ didn't make (it to) the concert.
　　 ◎ Ⓒ didn't get to the concert in time.
　　 ○ Ⓓ didn't make it for the concert.
　　 × Ⓔ didn't make it on the concert.

(b) 飛行機・電車のような動くもの
　　●遅れた事実のみを述べるとき
　　（私たちは8時の飛行機に乗り遅れたんです）
We ☆ Ⓐ missed the 8:00 flight.
　　 ◎ Ⓑ didn't make [catch] the 8:00 flight.
　　 ◎ Ⓒ were late for the 8:00 flight.
　　 ○ Ⓓ weren't on [in] time for the 8:00 flight.
　　 ○ Ⓔ didn't get to the airport on [in] time for the 8:00 flight.
　　 ○ Ⓕ didn't get to the 8:00 plane on time.
　　 ○ Ⓖ didn't get to the 8:00 flight on time.
　　 ○ Ⓗ didn't make it for [on] the 8:00 flight.
　　 △ Ⓘ didn't make it to the 8:00 flight.
　　 △ Ⓙ didn't get to the 8:00 plane [flight] in time.

　　●遅れている時間数を述べるとき
　　（7時の急行は事故のため15分遅れています）
The 7:00 express's ☆ Ⓐ 15 minutes late because of the accident.
　　　　　　　　　　 ◎ Ⓑ 15 minutes behind (the schedule) ...
　　　　　　　　　　 ◎ Ⓒ behind (the schedule) by 15 minutes ...
　　　　　　　　　　 ◎ Ⓓ delayed [overdue] by 15 minutes ...
　　　　　　　　　　 ○ Ⓔ late by 15 minutes ...
　　　　　　　　　　 ○ Ⓕ 15 minutes overdue ...
　　　　　　　　　　 ▽ Ⓖ 15 minutes delayed ...

17「ぎりぎりで」
　　（私は今朝7時の電車にぎりぎりで間に合ったんです）

Ⓐ just caught the 7:00 train this morning.
　◎ Ⓑ just barely caught the 7:00 train this morning.
　○ Ⓒ barely caught the 7:00 train this morning.
　○ Ⓓ narrowly caught the 7:00 train this morning.
　△ Ⓔ only just caught the 7:00 train this morning.
　△ Ⓕ only barely caught the 7:00 train this morning.
　△ Ⓖ caught the 7:00 train in the nick of time this morning.
〔注意〕上の表現は「やっと」「かろうじて」という日本語にもぴったり。

18 「今日中に」

(今日中に彼に連絡して下さい)
Please get in touch with him ◎ Ⓐ by tonight.
　　　　　　　　　　　　　　◎ Ⓑ by the end of the day.
　　　　　　　　　　　　　　○ Ⓒ before the day's through.
〔注意〕辞典に within (the course of) the day が出ているが使われていない。

19 「週末に（は）」

(a) 漠然と「週末に」と言う場合
(私たちは週末はおじさんの家にいます)
We're going to stay at my uncle's ◎ Ⓐ for the weekend.
　　　　　　　　　　　　　　　　 ○ Ⓑ over the weekend.
　　　　　　　　　　　　　　　　 △ Ⓒ on the weekend.
〔注意〕一般に「週末」と言えば，金曜の夜から日曜までを指す。

(b) 週末の中の「ある1日」を意味する場合
(私は週末にブルーミングデールでビルと偶然会いました)
I ran into Bill at Bloomingdale's ◎ Ⓐ over the weekend.
　　　　　　　　　　　　　　　　 △ Ⓑ on the weekend.

(c) 「毎週末」を意味する場合
(私は週末は駐車場の係員として働いています)
I work as a parking attendant ◎ Ⓐ on weekends.
　　　　　　　　　　　　　　　◎ Ⓑ on the weekends.
　　　　　　　　　　　　　　　○ Ⓒ on the weekend.

第4章
感情・気持に関する表現

1「(親・兄弟・姉妹・子供へ) 愛している」
　(お母さん，愛しています)
　　◎ Ⓐ Mom, I love you.
　　× Ⓑ Mom, I'm in love with you.

2「愛着がある」
　(私は故郷に強い愛着を持っています)
　　◎ Ⓐ I really love my hometown.
　　○ Ⓑ I'm really attached to my hometown.
　　△ Ⓒ I'm strongly [deeply] attached to my hometown.
　　△ Ⓓ I have [feel] a strong attachment for my hometown.

　[注意] ⒸⒹが辞典に出ているがときどきしか使われていない。Ⓐは辞典に出ていないが非常によく使われている。

3「うれしい」
(a)　同僚に話す場合
　　(ジェフ：君は仕事が速いってみんなが言ってるよ)
　　Jeff: Everybody's saying you're a fast worker.
　　(ジェラルド：うれしいよ)
　　Gerald:　◎ Ⓐ I'm glad [happy] to hear that.
　　　　　　◎ Ⓑ That's nice [good, great] to hear.
　　　　　　◎ Ⓒ It's nice [good] to hear that.
　　　　　　○ Ⓓ That makes me happy.

[33]

○ Ⓔ Nice to hear that.
△ Ⓕ Good to hear that.

(b) 強調して同僚に話す場合
(とてもうれしいよ)
◎ Ⓐ It's great to hear that.
◎ Ⓑ I'm really happy to hear that.
◎ Ⓒ I'm very happy to hear that.
○ Ⓓ I'm thrilled to hear that.
△ Ⓔ It's terrific to hear that.

4 「気分がいいんです」

(私は昇進したんです，だから気分がいいんです)
I've been promoted, so I feel ☆ Ⓐ great.
◎ Ⓑ good.
○ Ⓒ terrific.
○ Ⓓ incredible.
○ Ⓔ wonderful.
○ Ⓕ fantastic.

5 「怖い」

(a) 人が主語のとき
(母：お隣のご夫婦が昨夜殺されたのよ)
Mother: The couple next door were killed last night.
(娘：怖い)
Daughter: I'm ☆ Ⓐ scared.
◎ Ⓑ frightened.
◎ Ⓒ terrified.
○ Ⓓ afraid.
[注意] 怖さの程度はⒸが1番強い。ⒶⒷは同じ。Ⓓは1番弱い。

(b) 人が主語でないとき
(母：角のご夫婦が昨夜殺されたのよ)
Mother: The couple on the corner were killed last night.
(娘：怖い)
Daughter: That's ☆ Ⓐ scary.
◎ Ⓑ frightening.

　　　　　○ Ⓒ terrifying.
　[注意] 怖さの程度はⒸが1番強い。ⒶⒷは同じ。但しⒷは少し堅い響きがある。

6 「喉から手が出るほど欲しい」
　（私たちはあのお屋敷が喉から手が出るほど欲しいんです）
　◎ Ⓐ We want that mansion so badly it hurts.
　◎ Ⓑ We want that mansion so badly we can taste it.
　◎ Ⓒ We'd kill [die] for that mansion.
　◎ Ⓓ We're dying [anxious] to buy that mansion.
　○ Ⓔ We're eager [itching] to buy that mansion.

7 「…したくてたまらない」
(a)　どこかへ行きたいと述べる場合
　●計画がすでにあるとき
　（私たちは本当にフランスへ行きたくてたまらないんです）
　◎ Ⓐ We're really dying to go to France.
　◎ Ⓑ We can hardly wait to go …
　◎ Ⓒ We can't wait to go …
　○ Ⓓ We're really anxious [eager] to go …
　△ Ⓔ We're really itching to go …
　× Ⓕ We're really tickling [burning, impatient] to go …
　× Ⓖ We're really keen on going …
　[注意] (1) ⒻⒼが辞典に出ているが使われていない。
　(2) Ⓔは「すぐに」という響きが1番強い。
　●計画がないとき
　（私たちは本当にフランスへ行きたくてたまらないんです）
　We're really ◎ Ⓐ dying to go to France.
　　　　　　　○ Ⓑ anxious [eager] to go …
　　　　　　　△ Ⓒ itching to go …

(b)　人に会いたいと述べる場合
　●計画がすでにあるとき
　（私たちはあなたにとても会いたくてたまらないんです）
　◎ Ⓐ We can hardly wait to see you.
　◎ Ⓑ We can't wait to see you.
　◎ Ⓒ We're really dying to see you.

○ Ⓓ We're really anxious [eager] to see you.
△ Ⓔ We're really itching to see you.
● 計画がないとき
（私たちはあなたにとても会いたくてたまらないんです）
We're really ◎ Ⓐ dying to see you.
○ Ⓑ anxious [eager] to see you.
△ Ⓒ itching to see you.

8 「怒っている」
(a) 気分を害している
（マリアはリズに気分を害しているんです）
◎ Ⓐ Maria's upset with Liz.
◎ Ⓑ Maria isn't happy with Liz.

(b) むっとしている
（ボブは私が遅れたのでむっとしていました）
Bob was ◎ Ⓐ offended because I was late.
◎ Ⓑ put out ...
◎ Ⓒ miffed ...
◎ Ⓓ upset ...
◎ Ⓔ displeased ...
［注意］ⒶⒷはⒸⒹⒺより強い響きがある。

9 「怒って席を立つ」
（彼は怒って席を立ちました）
◎ Ⓐ He got angry and left his seat.
○ Ⓑ He left his seat in anger.
○ Ⓒ He left his seat in a rage.
△ Ⓓ He left his seat in his anger.
▽ Ⓔ He left his seat in his rage.

10 「かっとなる」
（彼はすぐかっとなるんです）
☆ Ⓐ He gets mad [pissed-off, angry] really easy.
◎ Ⓑ He gets mad [pissed-off, angry] really easily.
◎ Ⓒ He has a short fuse.
◎ Ⓓ He's really hot-tempered [quick-tempered, short-tempered].

第 4 章　感情・気持に関する表現

◎ Ⓔ He's really quick to lose his temper.
○ Ⓕ He's really quick to blow his top [cool, hit the ceiling, hit the roof, fly off the handle].
[注意] see red, fly into passion が辞典に出ているが使われていない。

11 「頭にくる」
（彼の横柄な態度は頭にくる）
His arrogant attitude ☆ Ⓐ drives me crazy.
　　　　　　　　　　　◎ Ⓑ drives me up the wall.
　　　　　　　　　　　◎ Ⓒ makes me crazy.
　　　　　　　　　　　◎ Ⓓ makes [drives] me nuts.
　　　　　　　　　　　○ Ⓔ makes me insane [looney].
　　　　　　　　　　　○ Ⓕ drives me to drink.
　　　　　　　　　　　△ Ⓖ makes me lunatic.
　　　　　　　　　　　△ Ⓗ makes me go off the deep end.

12 「気に障る」
（リンダの横柄な態度が気に障り始めているんです）
Linda's arrogant attitude's started to ☆ Ⓐ get on my nerves.
　　　　　　　　　　　　　　　　　　　☆ Ⓑ get to me.
　　　　　　　　　　　　　　　　　　　☆ Ⓒ bug [bother] me.
　　　　　　　　　　　　　　　　　　　○ Ⓓ annoy me.
　　　　　　　　　　　　　　　　　　　△ Ⓔ get under my skin.
　　　　　　　　　　　　　　　　　　　△ Ⓕ disturb [grate on] me.
[注意] 辞典に give [cause] me pain が出ているが使われていない。

13 「(忍耐が) 切れる」
（ボブはたぶんすぐ忍耐が切れるでしょう）
◎ Ⓐ Bob'll most likely run out of patience soon.
◎ Ⓑ Bob'll most likely be out of patience soon.
◎ Ⓒ Bob'll most likely lose his patience soon.
△ Ⓓ Bob's patience'll most likely be running out soon.

14 「くやしい」
(a) 感情的に述べる場合
（くやしい！）
☆ Ⓐ Damn it!

☆ ⓑ Damn!
　How ◎ ⓒ frustrating!
　　　　◎ ⓓ annoying!
　　　　◎ ⓔ irritating!
　　　　× ⓕ vexatious!
　　　　× ⓖ causing chagrin!
　［注意］ⓕⓖが辞典に出ているが使われていない。

(b)　誰がくやしいのかを述べる場合
　　（私はくやしいです）
　　☆ ⓐ I'm frustrated.
　　◎ ⓑ I'm feeling frustrated.
　　○ ⓒ I feel frustrated.
　　△ ⓓ I have frustration.
　　▽ ⓔ I have a frustration.
　　［注意］feel［be］chagrined［vexed］, have vexation が辞典に出ている
　　が使われていない。

15 「くやしくて」
　　（くやしくて彼は帽子を床にたたきつけた）
　　◎ ⓐ In his frustration he threw his cap on the floor.
　　× ⓑ In his vexation …
　　× ⓒ In the excess of his frustration …
　　× ⓓ In the excess of his vexation …
　　× ⓔ Out of chagrin, …
　　× ⓕ Out of vexation …
　　［注意］(1) 上の文は野球のチャンスで打てなかったときのくやしさ。
　　(2) ⓑⓒⓓⓔⓕは辞典に出ているが使われていない。

16 「反発する」
　　（もしあなたがそれを若い人たちに言えば彼らは反発するでしょう）
　　If you say that to young people, they'll
　　☆ ⓐ resent you.
　　◎ ⓑ feel resentment towards you.
　　○ ⓒ feel resentful of you.
　　○ ⓓ feel resentful towards you.

第4章　感情・気持に関する表現

17 「胸が詰まる」
（リンダは感動的な映画を見るといつも胸が詰まるんです）
Everytime Linda sees a touching movie,
　☆ Ⓐ she gets choked up.
　◎ Ⓑ she gets a lump in her throat.
　○ Ⓒ she chokes up.
　○ Ⓓ she has a lump in her throat.
　△ Ⓔ she feels a lump in her throat.
　× Ⓕ her throat gets choked up.

18 「傷つく」
（バーバラは傷つきやすいんです）
　☆ Ⓐ Barbara gets her feelings hurt easily.
　☆ Ⓑ Barbara gets hurt easily.
　☆ Ⓒ Barbara's feelings get hurt easily.
　◎ Ⓓ Barbara's feelings're easily hurt.
　◎ Ⓔ Barbara's really sensitive.

19 「舞い上がっている」
(a) 昇進・合格・成功
　●一般的に述べるとき
（ジェラルドは昇進したから舞い上がっているんです）
　☆ Ⓐ Gerald's excited because he got promoted.
　◎ Ⓑ Gerald's thrilled ...
　○ Ⓒ Gerald's in seventh heaven ...
　△ Ⓓ Gerald's beaming ...
　△ Ⓔ Gerald feels giddy [Gerald's giddy] ...
　× Ⓕ Gerald's beside himself ...
　× Ⓖ Gerald's overjoyed ...
　［注意］(1) Ⓖは主語が女性のときによく使われている。
(2) Ⓕは辞典に肯定的な内容で紹介されているが使われていない。否定的な内容ならよく使われている。
　●強く述べるとき
（フランクは昇進したからすごく舞い上がっているんです）
　☆ Ⓐ Frank's really excited because he got promoted.
　◎ Ⓑ Frank's really thrilled ...
　◎ Ⓒ Frank's ecstatic ...

◎ Ⓓ Frank's walking on air ...
　　　◎ Ⓔ Frank's on cloud nine ...
　　　○ Ⓕ Frank's walking on [in] the clouds ...
　　　○ Ⓖ Frank's head's in the clouds ...

(b)　異性関係で
　　●一般的に述べるとき
　　（スーザンはデートに誘われたから舞い上がっているんです）
　　☆ Ⓐ Susan's excited because she was asked out for a date.
　　◎ Ⓑ Susan's thrilled ...
　　○ Ⓒ Susan's in seventh heaven ...
　　○ Ⓓ Susan's beaming [overjoyed] ...
　　△ Ⓔ Susan feels giddy [Susan's giddy] ...
　　●強く述べるとき
　　（サラはデートに誘われたからすごく舞い上がっているんです）
　　☆ Ⓐ Sarah's really excited because she was asked out for a date.
　　◎ Ⓑ Sarah's really thrilled ...
　　◎ Ⓒ Sarah's ecstatic ...
　　◎ Ⓓ Sarah's walking on air ...
　　○ Ⓔ Sarah's walking on [in] the clouds ...
　　○ Ⓕ Sarah's mind's in the clouds ...
　　△ Ⓖ Sarah's on cloud nine ...

20「意気消沈している」
　　（最近彼は意気消沈しているんです）
　　These days ☆ Ⓐ he's depressed.
　　　　　　　 ☆ Ⓑ he's feeling down.
　　　　　　　 ◎ Ⓒ he's feeling blue.
　　　　　　　 ○ Ⓓ he's feeling low.
　　　　　　　 ○ Ⓔ he feels down.
　　　　　　　 ○ Ⓕ he has the blues.
　　　　　　　 ○ Ⓖ he's down [low].
　　　　　　　 ○ Ⓗ he feels blue.
　　　　　　　 × Ⓘ he has the dumps.

　　［注意］(1) Ⓘが辞典に出ているが使われていない。
　　(2) He's in low [bad, poor] spirits. He's melancholy. は辞典に出てい

[40]

第4章 感情・気持に関する表現

るがまれにしか使われていない。

21 「楽しむ」
(a) **クラシックコンサートのような知的な所へ行った場合**
　●普通に述べるとき
　（楽しかったです）
　◎ Ⓐ I had a good time.
　◎ Ⓑ I had a great time.
　○ Ⓒ It was enjoyable.
　○ Ⓓ I enjoyed myself.
　× Ⓔ I had fun.
　× Ⓕ It was fun.
　[注意]（1）ⒺⒻは知的なことには使われていない。
　（2）ⒸⒹは改まった響きがある。
　（3）ⒷのほうがⒶより少し強い。
　●強調して述べるとき
　（非常に楽しかったです）
　◎ Ⓐ It was really great [terrific, wonderful].
　◎ Ⓑ I had a really great [terrific, wonderful] time.
　○ Ⓒ It was really enjoyable.
　○ Ⓓ I really enjoyed myself.
　○ Ⓔ I really had a good time.
　○ Ⓕ It was really incredible.
　○ Ⓖ I had a really incredible time.
　[注意]（1）incredible が1番強く，wonderful, terrific, great の順で弱くなる。
　（2）ⒸⒹⒺは改まった響きがある。

(b) **スポーツ・ピクニック・ロックコンサート**
　●普通に述べるとき
　（楽しかったです）
　◎ Ⓐ I had a good time.
　◎ Ⓑ I had a great time.
　○ Ⓒ It was fun.
　○ Ⓓ I enjoyed myself.
　○ Ⓔ It was enjoyable.
　●強調して述べるとき

(とても楽しかったです)
◎ Ⓐ I had a really great time.
◎ Ⓑ I had a lot of fun.
◎ Ⓒ It was a lot of fun.
◎ Ⓓ It was really terrific.
◎ Ⓔ I had a blast.
◎ Ⓕ I had a ball.
[注意]ⒺⒻは約40歳以下の人の間で非常によく使われている。

(c) ハネムーンのような一生に一度という経験
(私たちはとても楽しかったです)
◎ Ⓐ We had the time of our lives.
◎ Ⓑ We had a really terrific time.
◎ Ⓒ We had a really great time.

22 「苦労する」
(a) 苦労したひとつの行為を述べるとき
(私たちは彼らを計画に参加するよう説得するのにすごく苦労したよ)
◎ Ⓐ We had a really hard time ［had a real problem, had a big problem, really had a problem］ talking them into our plan.
◎ Ⓑ We had a lot of ［a big, a real］ trouble talking them ...
◎ Ⓒ It was really tough ［hard］ to talk them ...
○ Ⓓ It was really difficult to talk them ...
○ Ⓔ It was very difficult to talk them ...

(b) 一連の苦労を述べるとき
(ジムは人生でいろいろ苦労をしました)
Jim's ◎ Ⓐ suffered a lot of hardships ［troubles］ in his life.
　　　◎ Ⓑ endured ...
　　　◎ Ⓒ undergone ...
　　　◎ Ⓓ lived through ...
　　　◎ Ⓔ gone through ...
　　　◎ Ⓕ experienced ...
　　　◎ Ⓖ met with ...
[注意]苦労の度合はⒶⒷが1番強い。ⒸⒹⒺが次に強く、ⒻⒼが1番弱い。

23 「尊敬する」

(a) 普通に述べる場合
 (私はリンカーン大統領を尊敬しています)
 I ☆ Ⓐ look up to President Lincoln.
  ◎ Ⓑ respect ...
  ◎ Ⓒ think a lot of ...
  ○ Ⓓ think highly of ...
  ○ Ⓔ have respect for ...
  △ Ⓕ have a respect for ...
  △ Ⓖ feel respect for ...
  △ Ⓗ think much of ...
 [注意] 辞典に feel a respect for が出ているが使われていない。

(b) 「非常に尊敬している」と述べる場合
 (私はリンカーン大統領を非常に尊敬しています)
 I ☆ Ⓐ really look up to President Lincoln.
  ◎ Ⓑ really respect ...
  ◎ Ⓒ think very highly of ...
  ◎ Ⓓ think really highly of ...
  ◎ Ⓔ think a lot of ...
  ◎ Ⓕ very much respect ...

24 「軽蔑する」

(a) 怒りの気持が入っている場合
 (ニールはグレッグとジェフを軽蔑しています)
 Neal ◎ Ⓐ despises Greg and Jeff.
     ◎ Ⓑ really hates Greg and Jeff.
 [注意] (1) despise＝look down on としている辞典があるが, 両者はイコールではない。
 (2) Ⓐのほうが Ⓑ より強い響きがある。従ってニュアンスを近づけるために really が必要になってくる。

(b) 怒りの気持がない場合
 (フランクはエリックとハウワドを軽蔑しているんです)
  ☆ Ⓐ Frank looks down on Eric and Howard.
  ☆ Ⓑ Frank doesn't think much of ...
  ◎ Ⓒ Frank has a low opinion on ...
  ○ Ⓓ Frank doesn't think highly [a lot] of ...

- ○ Ⓔ Frank thinks nothing [little] of ...
- ○ Ⓕ Frank's turning up his nose at ...
- △ Ⓖ Frank holds Eric and Howard in low regard.
- △ Ⓗ Frank has [feels] contempt for ...
- × Ⓘ Frank slights [disdains, scorns] ...
- × Ⓙ Frank holds Eric and Howard in contempt [scorn, low repute].
- × Ⓚ Frank thinks meanly [lightly, scorn] of ...
- × Ⓛ Frank holds Eric and Howard cheap.
- × Ⓜ Frank is treading Eric and Howard under foot.
- × Ⓝ Frank is scorning at ...
- × Ⓞ Frank brings Eric and Howard into contempt.
- × Ⓟ Frank has [feels] a contempt for ...
- × Ⓠ Frank has [feels] scorn for ...

［注意］Ⓘ〜Ⓠは辞典に出ているが，会話はもちろん，堅い文章英語でも現在は使われていない。

25 「恋しい」

(a) **物が手に入らないとき**

（ニューヨークにいる日本人：私は日本料理が恋しいんです）
- ◎ Ⓐ I miss Japanese food.
- ○ Ⓑ I'm homesick for Japanese food.
- △ Ⓒ I long for Japanese food.
- △ Ⓓ I'm longing for Japanese food.

［注意］yearn for, be yearning for が辞典に出ているがまれにしか使われていない。

(b) **人に会えないとき**

（私はアメリカにいる家族が恋しいんです）
- ◎ Ⓐ I miss my family in America.
- ○ Ⓑ I'm homesick for my family in America.
- △ Ⓒ I long for my family in America.
- △ Ⓓ I'm longing for my family in America.

［注意］上の文のように I miss my family [my boyfriend] in America. は非常によく使われているが恋しい対象を him, her のように代名詞を使うときは場所を示す in America を従えない。

第4章　感情・気持に関する表現

26「淋しい」
(私は彼と離婚したのでとても淋しいんです)
Since I got divorced from him, ☆ Ⓐ I'm really lonely.
　　　　　　　　　　　　　　 ☆ Ⓑ I feel really lonely.
　　　　　　　　　　　　　　 ◎ Ⓒ I'm feeling really lonely.
　　　　　　　　　　　　　　 ◎ Ⓓ I'm all alone.
　　　　　　　　　　　　　　 ○ Ⓔ I feel all alone.
　　　　　　　　　　　　　　 ○ Ⓕ I really feel lonely.
　　　　　　　　　　　　　　 △ Ⓖ I'm really lonesome.

27「心配させる」
(彼は子供のときから私をすごく心配させてきたんです)
He's been ◎ Ⓐ worrying me a lot since he was a kid.
　　　　　 ○ Ⓑ giving me a lot of worries ...
　　　　　 ○ Ⓒ making me really worried ...
　　　　　 ○ Ⓓ a real worry to me ...

28「心配する」
(a) 命令文のとき
(心配しないで，採用してもらえるよ)
　☆ Ⓐ Don't worry. You'll get the job.
　◎ Ⓑ Don't be worried. You'll ...
　○ Ⓒ Relax. You'll ...
　○ Ⓓ Take it easy. You'll ...
　△ Ⓔ Don't be concerned. You'll ...
　[注意] 辞典に Don't be anxious. が出ているが使われていない。

(b) 状態として述べるとき
(私たちはメアリーの安全が心配なんです)
　☆ Ⓐ We're worried about Mary's safety.
　◎ Ⓑ We worry about ...
　◎ Ⓒ We're concerned about ...
　○ Ⓓ We're concerned for ...
　× Ⓔ We're anxious about ...

(c) 待ち遠しいというニュアンスがあるとき
(息子はテストの結果が非常に心配だったので夜眠れなかったんです)

[45]

☆ Ⓐ My son was so anxious about the test results that he had a
　　◎ Ⓑ My son was so worried about ...
　　◎ Ⓒ My son worried about ...
　　○ Ⓓ My son was so concerned about ...
　　△ Ⓔ My son was so concerned for ...
sleepless night.

29 「心配性」
（彼は心配性なんです）
He's ☆ Ⓐ a worrier.
　　　　◎ Ⓑ a worrywart.
　　　　○ Ⓒ a born worrier.
　　　　○ Ⓓ a natural worrier.
［注意］辞典に He has a worrying personality ［nature］. が出ているがまれにしか使われていない。

30 「恥ずかしい」
(a) 失敗を見られるなどして「ばつが悪い」
（私たちは今日会合に遅れたんです。部屋に入ったときみんなが私たちを見たんです。本当に恥ずかしかったです）
　◎ We were late for the meeting today. When we got in the room, everybody looked at us. We were really embarrassed.

(b) 法律に違反して
（私はリンダの財布を盗んだんです。とても恥ずかしく思っています）
I stole Linda's wallet. ◎ Ⓐ I feel so ashamed.
　　　　　　　　　　　　◎ Ⓑ I'm so ashamed of myself.

(c) モラルに反したことをして
（私は先週浮気をしてしまったんです。本当に恥ずかしく思っています）
I cheated on my wife last week. ◎ Ⓐ I feel really ashamed.
　　　　　　　　　　　　　　　　◎ Ⓑ I'm really ashamed of myself.

(d) 自分に能力がないことに対して怒りの気持で
（私は司法試験にまた落ちてしまったんです。恥ずかしく思っています）
　◎ I've failed the bar exam again. I'm embarrassed.

(e) おどおどしたり，はにかみ・内気の「恥ずかしがり」
　　（ビルは恥ずかしくてリンダを映画に誘えないんです）
　　Bill's too ☆ Ⓐ shy to ask Linda to go to the movies.
　　　　　　　◎ Ⓑ embarrassed ...
　　　　　　　△ Ⓒ bashful [timid] ...
　　[注意] 語法辞典にはこのような場合は bashful を使うとあるが実際には shy, embarrassed, timid も使われている。

　　（マイクは恥ずかしがり屋で大勢の人の前でスピーチすることはできないんです）
　　Mike's too ☆ Ⓐ shy to make a speech before a large audience.
　　　　　　　◎ Ⓑ timid ...
　　　　　　　△ Ⓒ bashful ...

31 「誇りを持っている」

(a) 自分自身に対して
　　（ボブは自分自身に誇りを持っています）
　　◎ Ⓐ Bob's proud of himself.
　　◎ Ⓑ Bob take [have] pride in himself.
　　◎ Ⓒ Bob's proud the way he is.
　　◎ Ⓓ Bob's proud who he is.
　　◯ Ⓔ Bob's proud to be himself.
　　× Ⓕ Bob's proud he's himself.

(b) 現在の幸運・現在の状態に感謝して述べるとき
　　（ジムはイギリス人であることに誇りを持っています）
　　☆ Ⓐ Jim's proud to be British.
　　◎ Ⓑ Jim's proud of being British.
　　◎ Ⓒ Jim's proud he's British.
　　◯ Ⓓ Jim take pride in being British.
　　△ Ⓔ Jim has pride in being British.

(c) ずうっとやってきたことに対して
　　（あなたはずうっとやってきたことに誇りを持つべきです）
　　You should ☆ Ⓐ have pride in what you've been doing.
　　　　　　　◎ Ⓑ take pride in ...
　　　　　　　◎ Ⓒ be proud of ...

○ Ⓓ show pride in ...

(d) 達成した地位に対して
（私は通訳であることに誇りを持っています）
☆ Ⓐ I'm proud of being an interpreter.
◎ Ⓑ I'm proud to be an interpreter.
○ Ⓒ I'm proud of I'm an interpreter.
○ Ⓓ I take pride in being an interpreter.
△ Ⓔ I have pride in being an interpreter.

32 「優越感」
（エリックはグレッグに優越感を持っているんです）
Eric ☆ Ⓐ thinks he's better than Greg.
　　　◎ Ⓑ thinks he's superior to Greg.
　　　○ Ⓒ has a superiority complex towards ［to］ Greg.
　　　△ Ⓓ has a sense of superiority towards ［to］ Greg.
　　　▽ Ⓔ has a superiority complex with regard to Greg.
［注意］辞典にⒶⒷが出ていないが非常によく使われている。

33 「劣等感」
（エリックはピーターに劣等感を持っているんです）
◎ Ⓐ Eric thinks he isn't as good as Peter.
◎ Ⓑ Eric thinks he's worse than Peter.
◎ Ⓒ Eric thinks he's inferior to Peter.
◎ Ⓓ Eric thinks Peter's better than him.
○ Ⓔ Eric's intimidated by Peter.
○ Ⓕ Eric has an inferiority complex towards ［to］ Peter.
△ Ⓖ Eric has a sense of inferiority towards ［to］ Peter.

34 「期待する」
(a) 一般的に述べる場合
（私たちはあなたに大いに期待しています）
☆ Ⓐ We expect a lot from you.
◎ Ⓑ We're expecting a lot from you.
◎ Ⓒ We're expecting a great deal from you.
◎ Ⓓ We expect a great deal from you.
○ Ⓔ We expect a lot ［a great deal］ of you.

(b) 改まった言い方で述べる場合
(私たちはあなたに大いに期待しています)
We have ◎ Ⓐ high expectation of you.
○ Ⓑ high expectation from you.
△ Ⓒ a high expectation of you.
× Ⓓ a high expectation from you.

35 「心があったかい」
(上司は心があったかい人です)
☆ Ⓐ The boss's a nice [good] guy.
☆ Ⓑ The boss's a great guy.
○ Ⓒ The boss's a nice person.
○ Ⓓ The boss's a great person.
○ Ⓔ The boss's warm-hearted.
○ Ⓕ The boss has a warm heart.
[注意] ⒺⒻは女性が話し手なら◎で使われているが、男性が話し手なら△に下がる。男性はⒶⒷⒸⒹで普通表現する。女性がⒶⒷⒸⒹを使う頻度は○である。

36 「思いやりがある」
(彼は思いやりがあります)
He's ◎ Ⓐ thoughtful.
◎ Ⓑ considerate.
◎ Ⓒ all heart.
○ Ⓓ caring.
○ Ⓔ compassionate.
[注意] (1) be obliging が辞典に出ているが会話ではまれ。
(2) Ⓔが1番強い響きがあり、ⒶⒷⒸⒹはほぼ同じ。

37 「ずるい」
(彼はずるいよ)
He's ◎ Ⓐ sneaky.
○ Ⓑ scheming.
○ Ⓒ devious.
△ Ⓓ underhanded [cunning].
△ Ⓔ sly [slick].

［注意］辞典に crafty が出ているが最近はほとんど使われていない。

38 「卑劣な」
（ティムは卑劣な男だ）
Tim's ◎ Ⓐ a mean guy.
　　　 ○ Ⓑ a nasty guy.
　　　 △ Ⓒ a despicable guy.
　　　 ▽ Ⓓ a cowardly [contemptible] guy.
［注意］(1) Ⓓは辞典に出ているが会話ではまれ。
(2) 堅い文章英語ではⒸⒹもよく使われている。
(3) 卑劣さの度合はⒸが1番強い。Ⓑが2番，Ⓐが3番，Ⓓは4番。

39 「実に嫌な（不愉快な，うんざりさせられる）」
（彼は実に嫌な人です）
He's ◎ Ⓐ disgusting.
　　　◎ Ⓑ sicking.
　　　◎ Ⓒ obnoxious.
　　　◎ Ⓓ horrible.
　　　◎ Ⓔ terrible.
　　　◎ Ⓕ rude.
　　　○ Ⓖ offensive.
　　　○ Ⓗ nauseating.
　　　○ Ⓘ objectionable.
［注意］ⒹⒽが1番強く，ⒺⒻⒼが2番，ⒶⒸが3番，ⒷⒾが4番の順で弱くなる。

40 「ずうずうしい」
（彼は非常にずうずうしいんです）
◎ Ⓐ He has a lot of nerve.
◎ Ⓑ He's really impudent.
○ Ⓒ He's really nervy.
△ Ⓓ He has a lot of cheek.

41 「厚かましい」
（今日中に推せん状を私に書くことを期待するとはあなたは厚かましい）
It's ☆ Ⓐ rude of you to expect me to write a recommendation by today.

第4章 感情・気持に関する表現

　　◎ Ⓑ pushy of you ...
　　○ Ⓒ presumption [nervy] of you ...
　　△ Ⓓ impudent of you ...
[注意] 辞典に brassy, bold, bumptious, obtrusive が出ているが使われていない。

42 「恐怖症」
(a) 高所恐怖症
　　(ジムは高所恐怖症なんです)
　　☆ Ⓐ Jim's afraid [scared] of heights [high places].
　　◎ Ⓑ Jim hates heights [high places].
　　◎ Ⓒ Jim has acrophobia.
　　○ Ⓓ Jim has a fear of heights.
　　△ Ⓔ Jim has a phobia of heights.
[注意] 辞典に be heightsphobe, have a heightsphobia, have an acrophobia が出ているがまれ。

(b) 女性恐怖性
　　(ビルは女性恐怖症なんです)
　　☆ Ⓐ Bill's afraid of women.
　　◎ Ⓑ Bill's scared of ...
　　○ Ⓒ Bill has a fear of ...
　　○ Ⓓ Bill has phobia of ...
[注意] (1) 辞典に a woman phobe が出ているが使われていない。
(2) ⒷはⒶⒸⒹより強い。

(c) 対人恐怖症
　　(ジェフは対人恐怖症なんです)
　　☆ Ⓐ Jeff's afraid of people.
　　◎ Ⓑ Jeff has a fear of ...
　　○ Ⓒ Jeff fears people.
　　△ Ⓓ Jeff has anthropophobia.

(d) 閉所恐怖症
　　(リンダは閉所恐怖症なんです)
　　Linda ☆ Ⓐ has claustrophobia.
　　　　　☆ Ⓑ hates small spaces.

◎ ⓒ is claustrophobic.
　　　　◎ ⓓ hates closed places ［small places］.
　　　　△ ⓔ is afraid of closed spaces.
　　［注意］辞典に be a claustrophobe が出ているが会話ではまれ。

(e)　**ホモ恐怖症**
　　（マイクはホモ恐怖症なんです）
　　Mike ☆ Ⓐ hates ［is afraid of］ homosexuals.
　　　　◎ Ⓑ is scared of ［has a fear of］ homosexuals.
　　　　◎ ⓒ is a homophobic.
　　　　◯ ⓓ is a homophobe.

第5章 性質に関する表現

1 「私の性質」
(それは私の性質なんです)
That's ☆ Ⓐ the way I am.
　　　　◎ Ⓑ me.
　　　　○ Ⓒ my nature.

2 「明るい人」
(彼は明るい人です)
☆ Ⓐ He's a happy guy [person].
◎ Ⓑ He's a cheerful guy [person].
○ Ⓒ He has a cheerful personality [nature].
△ Ⓓ He has a sunny nature [disposition].
[注意] 辞典に be jovial [merry], be a chipper person が出ているが使われていない。

3 「社交的な」
(a) 努力するニュアンスの場合
(ビルは社交的です)
Bill's ☆ Ⓐ outgoing.
　　　 ◎ Ⓑ sociable.
　　　 ◎ Ⓒ a sociable guy.
　　　 ◎ Ⓓ a sociable [people] person.

(b) 努力でなく性質上

[53]

（ビルは社交的です）
Bill can ☆ Ⓐ get along with anybody.
　　　　　◎ Ⓑ hang around ...
　　　　　◎ Ⓒ hang out ...
　　　　　◎ Ⓓ socialize ...
　　　　　○ Ⓔ mix well ...

4 「八方美人」
（ピーターは八方美人です）
◎ Ⓐ Peter's two-faced.
○ Ⓑ Peter talks out of both sides of his mouth.
△ Ⓒ Peter's everybody's friend.
× Ⓓ Peter's double-faced ［double-tongued］.
［注意］(1) Ⓓが辞典に出ているが使われていない。
(2) Ⓒも辞典に出ているがときどき使われる程度。この表現は「みんなに好かれている」という肯定的な意味でなら非常によく使われている。

5 「社交的ではない」
（彼は社交的ではないんです）
☆ Ⓐ He isn't sociable.
◎ Ⓑ He isn't a sociable ［people］ person.
◎ Ⓒ He's unsociable.
◎ Ⓓ He's anti-social.
○ Ⓔ He's an unsociable person.
○ Ⓕ He doesn't mix well with people.
△ Ⓖ He's a bad mixer.

6 「接待が上手です」
（彼はパーティーで接待が上手です）
☆ Ⓐ He throws a great party.
◎ Ⓑ He's a good host.
◎ Ⓒ He can throw a great party.
○ Ⓓ He throws great parties.

7 「話好きの人」
（彼は話好きの人です）
☆ Ⓐ He's a good conversationalist.

第5章　性質に関する表現

◎ Ⓑ People like talking to him.
△ Ⓒ He's a good conversationist.
［注意］Ⓒが辞典に出ているがときどきしか使われていない。

8 「おしゃべり」
（彼はおしゃべりなんです）
☆ Ⓐ He never shuts up.
☆ Ⓑ He talks all the time.
◎ Ⓒ He never shuts his mouth.
○ Ⓓ He never closes his mouth.
△ Ⓔ He has a big mouth.
［注意］Ⓔは秘密を守れないという意味の「おしゃべり」では非常によく使われている。

9 「外向的」
（ビルは外向的です）
Bill's ☆ Ⓐ outgoing.
　　　 ◎ Ⓑ extroverted.
　　　 ○ Ⓒ an extroverted person.

10 「内向的」
（ビルは内向的です）
Bill's ☆ Ⓐ introverted.
　　　 ◎ Ⓑ an introverted person.
　　　 ◎ Ⓒ shy.
　　　 ○ Ⓓ a shy person.
［注意］辞典に introversive, introvertive が出ているが使われていない。

11 「きれい好き」
（彼女は非常にきれい好きなんです。お金を触った後ではいつも手を洗うんです）
☆ Ⓐ She's really clean, so she always washes her hands after
◎ Ⓑ She likes to be really clean, ...
○ Ⓒ She likes being really clean, ...
touching money.
［注意］(1) 辞典に She has clean habits. が出ているが使われていない。
(2) 日本語のきれい「好き」につられてⒶが対応しないように思われるかもし

[55]

れないが1番ぴったりする。

12 「純粋な」
（彼は純粋な人です）
He's ☆ Ⓐ innocent.
　　　 ◯ Ⓑ an innocent.
　　　 ◯ Ⓒ naive.
[注意]（1）Ⓒは「だまされやすい」という意味でもよく使われている。
（2）be pure-hearted, be genuine-hearted, be pure of heart が辞典に出ているが使用頻度は非常に低い。

13 「まじめである」
（彼はまじめな人なので決して不倫はしないでしょう）
　◎ Ⓐ He has high morals, he'd never cheat on his wife.
　◯ Ⓑ He's a very moral man, ...
　◯ Ⓒ He has strong values, ...
　◯ Ⓓ He has high ideals, ...
　× Ⓔ He's serious, ...
[注意] どの辞典にも serious＝「まじめ」と出ているが，serious にはこの意味はない。「真剣な」という意味である。

14 「無邪気な」
（彼はすごく無邪気なんです）
　☆ Ⓐ He's innocent.
　◎ Ⓑ He's naive.
　△ Ⓒ He's unsophisticated.
[注意] 辞典で無邪気な人をひくと名詞の an innocent が出ているが使われていない。He's pure-hearted. He has a pure heart. が出ているが使われていない。

15 「無頓着な」
（お金のことになるとリンダは無頓着です）
When it comes to money, ☆ Ⓐ Linda doesn't care.
　　　　　　　　　　　　 ◯ Ⓑ Linda's apathetic.
　　　　　　　　　　　　 ◯ Ⓒ Linda's indifferent.
　　　　　　　　　　　　 △ Ⓓ Linda's really unconcerned.
　　　　　　　　　　　　 △ Ⓔ Linda doesn't trouble herself.

16 「おっとりしている（のん気な）」
（リンダはおっとりしています）
Linda's ◎ Ⓐ laid-back.
　　　　◎ Ⓑ easy-going.
　　　　○ Ⓒ carefree.
　　　　△ Ⓓ happy-go-lucky.
［注意］Ⓐが 1 番強いニュアンスがある。Ⓓは「行き当たりばったり」という意味でも非常によく使われている。

17 「苦労性」
（母は苦労性なんです）
My mother ☆ Ⓐ takes things too seriously.
　　　　　☆ Ⓑ takes everything too seriously.
　　　　　◎ Ⓒ can't relax.

18 「気分屋」
（彼は気分屋です）
☆ Ⓐ He's moody.
◎ Ⓑ He has mood swings.
◎ Ⓒ He's a moody guy.
○ Ⓓ He's temperamental.
× Ⓔ He's a person [creature] of moods.
［注意］Ⓔが辞典に出ているが使われていない。

19 「横柄な」
（彼女は横柄です）
She's ◎ Ⓐ arrogant.
　　　○ Ⓑ on her high horse.
　　　○ Ⓒ self-important.
［注意］辞典に haughty が出ているが使われてもまれ。

20 「気取っている」
（バーバラは気取っている）
☆ Ⓐ Barbara's a snob.
☆ Ⓑ Barbara's stuck-up.
◎ Ⓒ Barbara's snobbish [snooty].

○ Ⓓ Barbara's snobby [uppity].
○ Ⓔ Barbara thinks she's all that.
△ Ⓕ Barbara has her nose in the air.
× Ⓖ Barbara's affected.
× Ⓗ Barbara's uppish [high-hatted, supercilious].
[注意] Ⓐは30歳以上、ⒷⒺは25歳以下の人の間でよく使われている。ⒻⒼは堅い文章英語ではよく使われている。

21 「ずけずけ言う」
(彼はいつもすべてのことにずけずけ言います)
☆ Ⓐ He's always outspoken about everything.
◎ Ⓑ He always speaks out about ...
◎ Ⓒ He always speaks his mind about ...
○ Ⓓ He always pulls no punches about ...

22 「ぶっきらぼうな」
(彼はすごくぶっきらぼうなんです)
☆ Ⓐ He talks very little.
◎ Ⓑ He's really blunt.
◎ Ⓒ He doesn't sugarcoat things [spare people's feelings].
○ Ⓓ He speaks very little.
○ Ⓔ He's really direct.

23 「残(冷)酷な」
(彼は残(冷)酷な人だ)
He's ☆ Ⓐ cold.
　　　◎ Ⓑ cruel.
　　　○ Ⓒ brutal.
　　　○ Ⓓ ruthless.
　　　○ Ⓔ heartless.
　　　△ Ⓕ merciless.
[注意] (1) 辞典に inhuman が出ているがまれにしか使われていない。
(2) Ⓒが1番強い響きがあり、Ⓓが2番、ⒶとⒺが3番、Ⓑが4番、Ⓕが5番。

24 「冷たい」
(彼は冷たい人です)
☆ Ⓐ He's cold.

第 5 章　性質に関する表現

◎ ⓑ He's cold-hearted.
○ ⓒ He has a cold heart.
○ ⓓ He has a cold personality.
[注意] be frost-hearted [frosty-hearted], have a frosty personality [nature, hearty] が辞典に出ているが使われていない。

25 「弱虫な（意気地のない）」
（ジミーは弱虫なんです）
Jimmy's ☆ Ⓐ a wimp.
　　　　◎ Ⓑ wimpy.
　　　　○ Ⓒ a weakling.
　　　　○ Ⓓ a sissy.
　　　　△ Ⓔ a weak guy.
　　　　△ Ⓕ wimpish.
[注意] 辞典に be sissy が出ているが使われていない。

26 「マザコン」
（ビルはマザコンです）
Bill's ◎ Ⓐ mother's running [controlling] his life.
　　　◎ Ⓑ mother runs his life.
　　　○ Ⓒ controlled by his mother.
　　　○ Ⓓ a mama's boy.
　　　○ Ⓔ tied to his mother's apron strings.
　　　× Ⓕ a mom's [mother's] boy.
[注意] (1) Ⓔは30歳以下の人の間ではときどきしか使われていない。
(2) 母親の言いなりになっている度合はⒶⒸの control が 1 番強く、ⒶⒷの run が 2 番、Ⓔは 3 番、Ⓓは 4 番でずっと弱くなる。

第6章
人間関係に関する表現

1 「失礼です」
(a) 一般的に述べる場合
   （あなたは私に失礼です）
   ☆ Ⓐ You're rude.
   ◎ Ⓑ You're rude to me.
   ◎ Ⓒ You were rude (to me).
   ○ Ⓓ You're impolite.
   △ Ⓔ You were impolite (to me).
   △ Ⓕ You're impolite to me.

(b) 強調して述べる場合
   （失礼ね）
   ☆ Ⓐ Excuse me!
   ☆ Ⓑ Excuse you!
   ◎ Ⓒ Sorry!
   ◎ Ⓓ I'm sorry!
   ［注意］(1) 相手が失礼であったときはいつでも使える。
   (2) Ⓐ～Ⓓいずれも文尾を上がり調子で言う
   (3) ⒷⒸはいずれの年代でも使われているが，特に30歳位の人の間で非常によく使われている

2 「礼儀」
(a) 「礼儀を知らない」と言う場合
   （ブライアンは礼儀を知らない）

◎ Ⓐ Brian has bad ［no］ manners.
◎ Ⓑ Brian's impolite.
○ Ⓒ Brian's bad-mannered ［ill-mannered, discourteous］.
［注意］Ⓑは中流の上，または上流階級の間で広く使われている。

(b) 「礼儀正しい」と言う場合
（ブライアンは礼儀正しいです）
☆ Ⓐ Brian has good manners.
◎ Ⓑ Brian's polite.
○ Ⓒ Brian's well-mannered.
○ Ⓓ Brian's courteous.
［注意］Ⓒは中流の上，または上流階級の成人の間で非常に広く使われている。

(c) 「礼儀上…する」という意味の場合
（ブライアンは礼儀上そう言ったんです）
Brian said it ◎ Ⓐ out of courtesy.
　　　　　　 ◎ Ⓑ to be polite.
　　　　　　 ○ Ⓒ out of politeness.
　　　　　　 △ Ⓓ to be courteous.

3 「行儀よくする」

(a) 子供に注意する場合
（今晩お客様が来たら行儀よくして下さい）
Please behave ◎ Ⓐ yourself when we have company this evening.
　　　　　　　 ○ Ⓑ when we have company …
　　　　　　　 × Ⓒ well when we have company …

(b) 成人（45歳位まで）の女性が述べる場合
（ビルは有名な政治家なので行儀よくしなければならないんです）
Since Bill's a famous politician, he has to
　　☆ Ⓐ be a good role model.
　　◎ Ⓑ behave himself.
　　◎ Ⓒ be careful of what he says and does.
　　○ Ⓓ behave ［watch himself］.
　　△ Ⓔ cover his ass ［butt］.
　　△ Ⓕ watch his P's and Q's.
　　× Ⓖ behave well.

(C) 成人（45歳位まで）の男性が述べる場合
　　（ビルは有名な政治家なので行儀よくしなければならないんです）
　　Since Bill's a famous politician, he has to
　　　☆ Ⓐ be a good role model.
　　　◎ Ⓑ cover his ass.
　　　◎ Ⓒ be careful of what he says and does.
　　　△ Ⓓ watch [behave] himself.
　　　△ Ⓔ behave.
　　　△ Ⓕ cover his butt.
　　　△ Ⓖ watch his P's and Q's.
　　　× Ⓗ behave well.

(c) 中年以上の女性が述べる場合
　　（ビルは有名な政治家なので行儀よくしなければならないんです）
　　Since Bill's a famous politician, he has to
　　　☆ Ⓐ be a good role model.
　　　◎ Ⓑ mind [watch] his P's and Q's.
　　　◎ Ⓒ be careful of what he says and does.
　　　◎ Ⓓ watch [behave] himself.
　　　○ Ⓔ behave.
　　　△ Ⓕ cover his ass [butt].

(d) 中年以上の男性が述べる場合
　　（ビルは有名な政治家なので行儀よくしなければならないんです）
　　Since Bill's a famous politician, he has to
　　　☆ Ⓐ be a good role model.
　　　◎ Ⓑ cover his ass.
　　　◎ Ⓒ be careful of what he says and does.
　　　◎ Ⓓ mind [watch] his P's and Q's.
　　　◎ Ⓔ watch himself.
　　　○ Ⓕ behave (himself).
　　　△ Ⓖ cover his butt.

4 「言葉遣い」
　　（言葉遣いに気をつけて下さい）
　　Please watch ☆ Ⓐ how you speak.

第6章　人間関係に関する表現

　　　◎ Ⓑ your language ［mouth, tongue］.
　　　◎ Ⓒ how you're speaking.
　　　○ Ⓓ how you're talking.
　　　○ Ⓕ how you talk.

5 「下品な言葉を使う」
　（彼は下品な言葉を使う）
　　☆ Ⓐ He has a foul mouth.
　　◎ Ⓑ He uses bad ［foul, vulgar］ language.
　　◎ Ⓒ He curses a lot.
　　◎ Ⓓ He has a dirty mouth.
　　◎ Ⓔ He uses dirty words.
　　○ Ⓕ He uses bad ［vulgar］ words.
　［注意］辞典に low-class ［coarse, indecent］ words が出ているが使われていない。

6 「ほめる」
(a)　普通に述べる場合
　（ポールはあなたのことをほめていました）
　Paul said ◎ Ⓐ great things about you.
　　　　　　◎ Ⓑ terrific ［fantastic, wonderful］ things ...
　　　　　　◎ Ⓒ incredible things ...
　　　　　　◎ Ⓓ good things ...
　　　　　　◎ Ⓔ great stuff ...
　　　　　　○ Ⓕ terrific ［fantastic, wonderful］ stuff ...
　　　　　　○ Ⓖ incredible stuff ...
　　　　　　○ Ⓗ good stuff ...
　［注意］ほめる強さはⒸⒼが1番強く，ⒷⒻが2番，ⒶⒺが3番，ⒹⒽが4番。

(b)　改まった調子で述べる場合
　（ポールはあなたのことをほめていました）
　Paul ☆ Ⓐ said good things about you.
　　　　◎ Ⓑ spoke well of you.
　　　　◎ Ⓒ spoke ［talked］ highly of you.
　　　　○ Ⓓ spoke ［talked］ good of you.
　　　　△ Ⓔ praised you.
　［注意］ほめている強さはⒸが1番強い。

(c) 強めて述べている場合
　　（ポールはあなたのことをすごくほめていました）
　　Paul ☆ ⒶＡ said a lot of good things about you.
　　　　☆ Ⓑ really said good things ...
　　　　◎ Ⓒ really said great things ...
　　　　◎ Ⓓ really said incredible [terrific, fantastic, wonderful]
　　　　　　　things ...
　　　　◎ Ⓔ said a lot of good stuff ...
　　　　◎ Ⓕ really said terrific [incredible] stuff ...

7 「悪口を言う」

(a) 普通に述べる場合
　　（リンダはビルの悪口を言っていましたよ）
　　Linda ☆ Ⓐ said bad things about Bill.
　　　　☆ Ⓑ bad-mouthed Bill.
　　　　◎ Ⓒ said horrible [terrible] things about ...
　　　　◎ Ⓓ spoke [talked] bad about ...
　　　　◎ Ⓔ talked about Bill behind his back.
　　　　○ Ⓕ spoke [talked] badly about ...
　　　　○ Ⓖ said bad [horrible, terrible] stuff about ...
　　　　△ Ⓗ said awful things about ...
　　　　△ Ⓘ spoke horribly [terribly] about ...
　　　　△ Ⓙ talked horribly [terribly, shit] about ...
　　　　× Ⓚ spoke ill of ...
　　［注意］Ⓚは辞典に出ているが使われていない。

(b) 強調して述べる場合
　　（リンダはすごくビルの悪口を言っていましたよ）
　　Linda ☆ Ⓐ said a lot of bad things about Bill.
　　　　☆ Ⓑ really said bad things about ...
　　　　☆ Ⓒ really bad-mouthed Bill.
　　　　◎ Ⓓ said a lot of horrible [terrible] things about ...
　　　　◎ Ⓔ talked [spoke] really bad about ...
　　　　◎ Ⓕ really talked [spoke] bad about ...
　　　　◎ Ⓖ really talked about Bill behind his back.
　　　　○ Ⓗ said a lot of bad [terrible, awful] stuff about ...

第6章　人間関係に関する表現

8 「告げ口する」
(a) 子供の場合

（ニールが僕のことを父さんに告げ口したんだ）

Neal ◎ Ⓐ went to Dad and told on me.
　　 ◎ Ⓑ went to Dad and tattled on me.
　　 ○ Ⓒ went to Dad and squealed on me.
　　 ○ Ⓓ went to Dad and ratted on me.
　　 △ Ⓔ told [tattled] on me to Dad.

9 「ごますり」
(a) 下品な表現

（グレッグはごますりだ）

◎ Ⓐ Greg kisses his boss's ass.
◎ Ⓑ Greg's an ass-kisser.
○ Ⓒ Greg's a butt-kisser.
○ Ⓓ Greg's a kiss ass.

［注意］(1) a butt-kiss が辞典に出ているが使われていない。
(2) ⒶⒷⒸⒹは下品な表現であるが, 親しい者同士, またはかしこまって話す必要がないときは, 教育レベルに関係なくよく使われている。

(b) 下品でない表現

（ロンはごますりだ）

◎ Ⓐ Ron kisses up to his boss.
◎ Ⓑ Ron brown-noses.
◎ Ⓒ Ron's a brown-noser.
○ Ⓓ Ron brown-noses (to) his boss.
○ Ⓔ Ron plays up to his boss.
○ Ⓕ Ron butters up his boss.
▽ Ⓖ Ron's a brown-nose.

(c) 文章で使われる表現

（アランはごますりだ）

◎ Ⓐ Alan's an apple-polisher.
△ Ⓑ Alan curries favor with his boss.
▽ Ⓒ Alan toadies his boss.
▽ Ⓓ Alan plays the sycophant to his boss.

10「悪気はなかった」
(a) 普通に述べる場合
   (彼には悪気はなかったんです)
   ☆ Ⓐ His heart was in the right place.
   ◎ Ⓑ He didn't mean any harm.
   ◎ Ⓒ He meant no harm [offense].
   ○ Ⓓ His intentions were good.
   ○ Ⓔ He didn't intend any harm.

(b) 強調して述べるとき
   (彼には全く悪気はなかったんです)
   ☆ Ⓐ His intentions were really good.
   ◎ Ⓑ His intentions were entirely [totally, absolutely, completely, very, a hundred percent] good.
   ◎ Ⓒ He didn't mean any harm at all.
   ◎ Ⓓ He meant no harm at all.
   ◎ Ⓔ His intentions were quite good.
   ○ Ⓕ No offense was meant at all.
   ○ Ⓖ He didn't mean any harm whatsoever [in the least].
   [注意] ⒶⒷのほうがⒸⒹⒺⒻⒼより語調は強い。

11「せんさくがましい」
   (彼女はすごくせんさくがましいんです)
   ◎ Ⓐ She's really nosey.
   ◎ Ⓑ She gets into other people's businsess.
   ◎ Ⓒ She's such a snoop.
   ○ Ⓓ She pries into other people's business.
   ○ Ⓔ She pokes into other people's business.
   ○ Ⓕ She digs into other people's business.
   △ Ⓖ She's really snoopy.

12「口やかましい」
   (私が子供のとき母は食事の作法に口やかましかったんです)
   My mother was
      ☆ Ⓐ particular about table manners when I was a kid.
      ◎ Ⓑ picky ...

第 6 章　人間関係に関する表現

　　○ ⓒ fussy ...
　　△ ⓓ fastidious ...

13 「そっけない」
（銀行の窓口の係の人は私にそっけなかったんです）
The bank teller was ☆ ⓐ rude to me.
　　　　　　　　　◎ ⓑ short with me.
　　　　　　　　　◎ ⓒ snappy to me.
　　　　　　　　　○ ⓓ abrupt [snippy] to me.
　　　　　　　　　△ ⓔ curt to me.
[注意] 辞典に be gruff [terse] が出ているが使われていない。

14 「だます」
(a) 「だます」行為を述べる場合
（彼は私たちをだまそうとしているんです）
He's trying to ☆ ⓐ cheat us [rip us off].
　　　　　　　◎ ⓑ trick us [con us, gyp us, screw us].
　　　　　　　○ ⓒ fuck us [pull a fast one, pull a fast one on us].
　　　　　　　△ ⓓ deceive [bamboozle, swindle] us.
　　　　　　　△ ⓔ pull the wool of [over] our eyes.
[注意] ⓓⓔの5つの表現は人により△から○になる。

(b)　だまして何かを巻きあげる場合
（ビルとデイヴィッドは私をだましてお金を巻きあげようとしたんです）
Bill and David tried to
　☆ ⓐ rip me off.
　◎ ⓑ rip [cheat, screw] me out of my money.
　○ ⓒ con [fuck, gyp] me out of money.
　○ ⓓ bilk [milk, bamboozle] me out of money.
　△ ⓔ wheedle [dupe, hustle, swindle] me out of my money.
　× ⓕ cajole [fool, do, outsmart] me out of my money.
[注意] (1) bilk, milk, gyp は少しずつのニュアンスが強い。
(2) ⓕが辞典に出ているが使われていない。

(c)　「何に」だますかを明示して述べる場合
（ビルは私をだましてポンコツ車を買わせたんです）
Bill ☆ ⓐ talked [tricked] me into buying his piece of junk.

◎ Ⓑ conned me into ...
○ Ⓒ hustled [fooled] me into ...
△ Ⓓ duped me into ...
△ Ⓔ deceived me into ...

15 「だまされやすい」
（彼はだまされやすいんです）
He's ☆ Ⓐ gullible.
　　　◎ Ⓑ easily fooled.
　　　○ Ⓒ easily deceived.
　　　○ Ⓓ naive.
［注意］Ⓐが1番強いニュアンスがある。

16 「つけ込む」
（私は彼らの無知につけ込みたくないんです）
I don't want to
　　◎ Ⓐ take advantage of their ignorance.
　　○ Ⓑ play on [exploit] their ...
　　△ Ⓒ capitalize [cash in] on their ...
　　× Ⓓ presume on [impose on, practice on, trespass upon] their ...
　　× Ⓔ avail myself of their ...
　　× Ⓕ make advantage of their ...
［注意］(1) Ⓒの cash in は金銭的ニュアンスがはっきりしているときにのみ使われている。
(2) ⓄⒺⒻが辞典に出ているが使われていない。

17 「うぬぼれる」
(a) **動作を表す**
（そんなことをしたらポールをうぬぼれさせるだけですよ）
That'll only ◎ Ⓐ give Paul a bighead.
　　　　　　◎ Ⓑ go to Paul's head.
　　　　　　◎ Ⓒ make Paul get a bighead.
　　　　　　△ Ⓓ make Paul big-headed [conceited].

(b) **状態を表す**
（ポールはうぬぼれている）

第 6 章　人間関係に関する表現

◎ Ⓐ Paul's cocky [conceited].
◎ Ⓑ Paul's stuck on himself.
◎ Ⓒ Paul has a bighead.
○ Ⓓ Paul's big-headed.
△ Ⓔ Paul has a swelled head.

18 「好感を持っている」
(リンダは私たちに好感を持っているようだね)
It seems like Linda ☆ Ⓐ thinks good of us.
　　　　　　　　　　 ◎ Ⓑ thinks good about us.
　　　　　　　　　　 ○ Ⓒ holds good feelings towards us.
　　　　　　　　　　 ○ Ⓓ thinks well of us.
　　　　　　　　　　 ○ Ⓔ has good feelings towards us.
　　　　　　　　　　 ○ Ⓕ has a good impression of us.
　　　　　　　　　　 △ Ⓖ thinks well about us.

19 「好感を持っていない（よく思っていない）」
(リンダは私たちに好感を持っていないようだね)
It seems like Linda ☆ Ⓐ thinks bad about us.
　　　　　　　　　　 ◎ Ⓑ thinks bad of us.
　　　　　　　　　　 ◎ Ⓒ thinks badly about [of] us.
　　　　　　　　　　 ○ Ⓓ holds bad feelings towards us.
　　　　　　　　　　 ○ Ⓔ has bad feelings towards us.
　　　　　　　　　　 ○ Ⓕ has a bad impress of us.

20 「悪く思う」
(住宅ローンの保証人になれないけど悪く思わないでくれ)
I can't cosign for your home loan but don't
　　　☆ Ⓐ hate me.
　　　☆ Ⓑ be mad [angry] at me.
　　　○ Ⓒ resent me.
　　　◎ Ⓓ think bad about [of] me.
　　　◎ Ⓔ think badly about [of] me.
　　　◎ Ⓕ hold it against me.
　　　○ Ⓖ hold a grudge against me.
　　　△ Ⓗ be resentful of me.
［注意］悪く思う強さはⒶが1番，ⒷⒸが2番，ⒺⒻが3番，ⒼⒽが4番，Ⓓ

は1番弱い。

21 「人（みんな）に好かれる」
(スティーヴは人に好かれる人です)
☆ Ⓐ Steve's a really likable guy.
☆ Ⓑ Everybody really likes Steve.
◎ Ⓒ Steve's a really popular guy.
[注意]「人に好感を持たれる人」などの日本語にも相当する。

22 「気まずいんです」
(私は先日上司と激しい口論をしたので気まずいんです)
I had a fierce argument with my boss the other day, so
　◎ Ⓐ I feel uncomfortable working with him.
　◎ Ⓑ I don't feel comfortable working ...
　◎ Ⓒ I don't feel good about working ...
　◎ Ⓓ I feel funny working ...
　◯ Ⓔ I feel strange working ...
　◯ Ⓕ I feel awkward working ...

23 「（同性同士が）仲直りする」
(デイヴィッドとティムはまもなく仲直りするでしょう)
David and Tim'll ◎ Ⓐ settle their differences soon.
　　　　　　　　　◎ Ⓑ work things out soon.
　　　　　　　　　◯ Ⓒ patch things up soon.
　　　　　　　　　◯ Ⓓ make up [reconcile] soon.
　　　　　　　　　◯ Ⓔ bury the hatchet soon.
　　　　　　　　　△ Ⓕ get reconciled soon.
　　　　　　　　　× Ⓖ get back together soon.
[注意] Ⓓの make up は女性同士の場合には非常によく使われている。

24 「支える」
(a) **精神的に**
(私が交通事故で夫を失ったとき，とてもさびしかったんです。ナンシーはそんな私をとても支えてくれたんです)
When I lost my husband in the car wreck, I felt really lonely.
Nancy was really ☆ Ⓐ supportive to [of] me.
　　　　　　　　　◎ Ⓑ supporting [encouraging] me.

　　　　　　　○ Ⓒ comforting me.
　　　　　　　△ Ⓓ propping me up.
　　　　　　　△ Ⓔ backing me (up).

(b) 士気
　　(私たちは彼らの士気を支えなければならない)
　　We have to ◎ Ⓐ keep up their morale.
　　　　　　　 ◎ Ⓑ support their morale.
　　　　　　　 △ Ⓒ hold up their morale.
　　　　　　　 ▽ Ⓓ prop [prop up, back up] their morale.

25 「裏切る」
　　(私たちはデイヴィッドが裏切ったことを許せない)
　　We can't forgive David for ☆ Ⓐ betraying [double-crossing] us.
　　　　　　　　　　　　　　　 ◎ Ⓑ selling out on us.
　　　　　　　　　　　　　　　 ○ Ⓒ going back on us.
　　　　　　　　　　　　　　　 △ Ⓓ selling us down the river.
　　　　　　　　　　　　　　　 △ Ⓔ turning traitor.
　　［注意］Ⓔは us が不要。

26 「遠ざける」
　　(リンダの横柄な態度が大勢の人を遠ざけているんです)
　　Linda's arrogant attitude ☆ Ⓐ turns off a lot of people.
　　　　　　　　　　　　　　　◎ Ⓑ alienates a lot of people.
　　　　　　　　　　　　　　　○ Ⓒ separates her from a lot of people.
　　　　　　　　　　　　　　　△ Ⓓ cuts off [estranges] a lot of people.
　　［注意］辞典に turn away が出ているが使われてもまれ。

27 「自業自得」
　　(自業自得だね)
　　☆ Ⓐ You asked for it.
　　○ Ⓑ You had it coming (to you).
　　○ Ⓒ That [It] serves you right.
　　○ Ⓓ You deserve it.
　　○ Ⓔ You deserve that.

28 「見栄」

(彼は見栄のためにベンツを買ったんです)
He bought a Mercedes ☆ Ⓐ just to show off [just for show].
　　　　　　　　　　 ☆ Ⓑ just to make himself look good.
　　　　　　　　　　 ◎ Ⓒ to show off [for show].
[注意] 辞典に out of vanity が出ているが使われていない。

29 「見栄を張る」
(a) 2人称のことを述べる場合
　(見栄を張るな)
　Don't ☆ Ⓐ try to make yourself look better than you are.
　　　　 ◎ Ⓑ try to make yourself look good.
　　　　 ◎ Ⓒ try to put up a front.
　　　　 △ Ⓓ try to put on airs.
　[注意] 辞典に keep up appearances, be vainglorious, be pretentious が出ているが使われていない。

(b) 3人称のことを述べる場合
　(シィンディは見栄を張るためにベンツを買ったんです)
　Cindy bought a Mercedes
　　　☆ Ⓐ to make herself look better than she is.
　　　◎ Ⓑ to make herself look good.
　　　△ Ⓒ to keep up appearances.
　[注意] cut a dash, cut a wide swath が辞典に出ているが使われていない。

30 「行動力のある人」
　(ポールは行動力があります)
　Paul's ☆ Ⓐ a man of action.
　　　　 ◎ Ⓑ a go-getter.
　　　　 ○ Ⓒ a self-starter.
　　　　 ○ Ⓓ a doer.
　[注意] Ⓓは地域によって使用頻度は変わる。

31 「行動が速い」
　(彼は決定をしなければならないときはいつも行動が速いんです)
　Whenever he has to make decisions, ☆ Ⓐ he acts fast.
　　　　　　　　　　　　　　　　　　 ◎ Ⓑ he acts quick.
　　　　　　　　　　　　　　　　　　 ○ Ⓒ he's fast in action.

第6章　人間関係に関する表現

　　　　○ Ⓓ he acts quickly.
　　　　△ Ⓔ he's quick in action.

32 「口先だけ」
　　（ジムは口先だけです）
　　Jim's ◎ Ⓐ all talk and no action.
　　　　 ◎ Ⓑ all talk.
　　　　 ○ Ⓒ just a talker.

33 「無口です」
　　（彼は無口です）
　　　☆ Ⓐ He doesn't say very much.
　　　☆ Ⓑ He doesn't talk very much.
　　　☆ Ⓒ He doesn't say a lot.
　　　◎ Ⓓ He talks very little.
　　　○ Ⓔ He's a man of few words.
　　［注意］(1) 辞典に He's a silent man ［a quiet man, a man of silence］. He's dumb as an oyster. He doesn't have a word to throw a dog. が出ているが使われていない。
　　(2) Ⓔは普段はあまり話さないが「話すと傾聴に値することを言う人」の意味では非常によく使われている。

34 「一匹狼」
(a) **一般的に述べる場合**
　　（彼は一匹狼です）
　　He's ◎ Ⓐ a maverick.
　　　　 × Ⓑ a lone wolf.
　　　　 × Ⓒ a loner.
　　［注意］(1) ⒷⒸが辞典に出ているが使われていない。
　　(2) Ⓒは「他人と付き合うのが好きではない」「親しい友人はいない」という意味ではよく使われている。

(b) **政治家**
　　（彼は一匹狼の政治家です）
　　He's ◎ Ⓐ a maverick as a politician.
　　　　 × Ⓑ a lone wolf politician.
　　　　 × Ⓒ a lone wolf as a politician.

[注意] ⒷⒸが辞典に出ているが使われていない。

35 「いじめる」
(a) 深刻に
　　（みんなジェフの訛りをいじめたんです）
　　Everybody ◎ Ⓐ picked on Jeff's accent.
　　　　　　　◎ Ⓑ picked on Jeff about his accent.
　　　　　　　◯ Ⓒ picked on Jeff for his accent.
　　　　　　　△ Ⓓ pestered Jeff about his accent.

(b) 軽い気持で
　　（みんなディヴィッドの訛りをいじめたんです）
　　Everybody ◎ Ⓐ teased David about his accent.
　　　　　　　◎ Ⓑ bugged David about his accent.
　　　　　　　◎ Ⓒ poked fun at David's accent.
　　　　　　　◎ Ⓓ made fun of David's accent.
　　　　　　　△ Ⓔ needled David about his accent.

36 「水をさす」
(a) 人間関係
　　（リズは私たちの関係に水をさそうとしている）
　　Liz's trying to
　　　　☆ Ⓐ come between us.
　　　　◎ Ⓑ break us up.
　　　　◯ Ⓒ put a barrier between us.
　　　　◯ Ⓓ spoil our relationship.
　　　　◯ Ⓔ alienate us from each other.
　　　　△ Ⓕ sour our relationship.
　　　　△ Ⓖ alienate me from you.
　　　　△ Ⓗ throw cold water [a wet blanket] on our relationship.
　　　　△ Ⓘ throw a wrench into our relationship.
　　[注意] (1) 辞典に estrange, dash cold water, throw a chill が出ているが使われていない。
　　　　　(2) Ⓗは約45才以上の人にはときどき使われている。60歳以上なら普通に使われているが若い人たちの間では使われていない。

(b) 博士号・弁護士の資格などを取ろうとしている努力を伴う計画・夢など

(ボブが博士号を取ろうとしていることに水をささないで下さい)
Don't ◎ Ⓐ discourage Bob from getting his Ph. D.
　　　 △ Ⓑ get ［make］ Bob discouraged from ...
　　　 △ Ⓒ get ［bring］ Bob down from ...
［注意］ⒷⒸは人によってはまれにしか使われていない。従って相手が使ったときの知識としてインプットしておくべきだが，自分から使うことは勧めない。

37 「なれなれしい」
(a) 一般的に述べる場合
（ブライアンは私になれなれしいんです）
Brian's ◎ Ⓐ too friendly with me.
　　　　◎ Ⓑ too friendly to me.
　　　　○ Ⓒ overly-friendly with me.
　　　　○ Ⓓ overly-friendly to me.

(b) 特に性的ななれなれしさを表す場合
●その場限りのとき
（私になれなれしくするのをやめて下さい）
Stop ◎ Ⓐ hitting on me.
　　　◎ Ⓑ getting fresh with me.
　　　◎ Ⓒ making passes at me.
　　　△ Ⓓ making advances at ［towards］ me.
　　　× Ⓔ giving ［making］ attentions to me.
［注意］(1) Ⓔが辞典に出ているが使われていない。
(2) なれなれしさの程度はⒶが1番強い。Ⓑが2番，Ⓒが3番。
●繰り返し起こるとき
（ブライアンは毎日私になれなれしいんです）
Brian ◎ Ⓐ hits on ［gets fresh with］ me every day.
　　　 ◎ Ⓑ makes passes at me ...
　　　 △ Ⓒ makes advances at ［towards］ me ...
　　　 × Ⓓ makes an advance towards me ...

38 「聞き覚えがある」
（その名前は聞き覚えがある）
◎ Ⓐ That name rings a bell.
◎ Ⓑ That name sounds familiar.
◎ Ⓒ That name is familiar.

◎ ⒟ I think I remember that name.
○ ⒠ That name clicks.
○ ⒡ That name seems familiar.
△ ⒢ I feel I remember that name.

39 「秘密」
(a) 「秘密を守る」と言う場合
(これは秘密にしておいて下さい)
Please keep this ◎ ⒜ a secret.
○ ⒝ quiet.
○ ⒞ secret [confidential].
○ ⒟ under your hat.
○ ⒠ to yourself.
[注意] private, dark, under your bonnet [derby, Stetson], under wraps が辞典に出ているが使われていない。

(b) 「秘密を漏らす」と言う場合
(ジェフが秘密を漏らしたのかもしれません)
Jeff may've ◎ ⒜ let the cat out of the bag.
○ ⒝ spilled the beans.
○ ⒞ let the secret out.
○ ⒟ given the secret away.
○ ⒠ leaked the secret.
○ ⒡ betrayed the secret.
[注意] ⒜は1番深刻でないという響きがある。⒝がそれに続く，⒞⒟はほぼ同じで⒜⒝⒞⒟いずれも意図的でないという響きがあるのに対して⒠は意図的に漏らしたことの見返りがあったニュアンスがある。⒡は秘密を漏らさないと約束したニュアンスがある。

40 「評価する」
(a) 過大評価する場合
(私のことを過大評価しないで下さい)
Don't ◎ ⒜ overestimate me.
○ ⒝ overrate me.
△ ⒞ make [think] too much of me.
△ ⒟ overvalue me.

(b) **過小評価する場合**
　　（ジムを過小評価してはだめですよ）
　　Don't ◎ Ⓐ underestimate Jim.
　　　　　◎ Ⓑ underrate Jim.
　　　　　○ Ⓒ minimize Jim.
　　　　　○ Ⓓ undervalue Jim.
　　　　　○ Ⓔ belittle Jim.

第7章

容姿に関する表現

1 「上品です」
(a) **女性**
(彼の奥さんは上品です)
☆ Ⓐ His wife has style.
☆ Ⓑ His wife has class.
◎ Ⓒ His wife's classy.
◎ Ⓓ His wife's stylish.
◎ Ⓔ His wife's sophisticated.
◎ Ⓕ His wife's graceful.
○ Ⓖ his wife has grace.
○ Ⓗ His wife's elegant.
○ Ⓘ His wife's polished [refined].
○ Ⓙ His wife's distinguished.

[注意] ⒶⒹは容姿・服装・スタイル・身のこなし、ⒷⒸは容姿・服装・スタイル・身のこなしにも言及しているが態度・振舞いのことに1番強く言及している。Ⓔは服装を含めた多くのものに対して趣味がよく磨かれていて、知性を強く感じさせるという意味。ⒻⒼは歩き方・食事の仕方・話し方などの身のこなし方に言及している。Ⓗは容姿・服装・ヘアスタイル・身のこなし方・マナー・知性など広く言及している。教育レベルの高い人の間では非常によく使われている。Ⓘはマナー・服装の身につけ方。Ⓙは仕事上で成功しているというニュアンスが強い。従って、約45歳以上の人に言及するときに使われる。

(b) **男性**
(うちの上司は上品です)

☆ Ⓐ Our boss has style [class].
◎ Ⓑ Our boss's stylish [classy, sophisticated, distinguished].
○ Ⓒ Our boss's polished [elegant, refined].

2 「すらっとしている」
(a) **女性の場合**
(キャロルはすらっとしている)
Carol's ◎ Ⓐ skinny.
　　　　○ Ⓑ trim.
　　　　△ Ⓒ slim [slender, thin].
[注意] (1) Ⓐは「やせこけている」という意味でもよく使われている。どちらであるかは文脈による。
(2) Ⓒは中年以上の人の間では非常によく使われている。

(b) **男性の場合**
(ティムはすらっとしている)
Tim's ◎ Ⓐ skinny.
　　　◎ Ⓑ thin.
　　　○ Ⓒ slim.
　　　△ Ⓓ trim.

3 「セックスアピール」
(a) **「ある」と述べる場合**
　●くだけた会話で
(ブライアンはセックスアピールがあります)
◎ Ⓐ Brian turns me on.
◎ Ⓑ Brian's hot.
◎ Ⓒ Brian's sexy to me.
△ Ⓓ Brian's hot stuff to me.
× Ⓔ Brian's hot to me.
　●かしこまって述べるとき
(ブライアンはセックスアピールがあります)
◎ Ⓐ Brian's physically attractive to me.
◎ Ⓑ Brian's sexually attractive to me.
◎ Ⓒ I'm physically attracted to Brian.
◎ Ⓓ I'm sexually attracted to Brian.
○ Ⓔ Brian appeals to me physically [sexually].

[注意] 友人同士の会話でもⒶ〜Ⓔがときどき使われることがある。

(b) 「ない」と述べる場合
　● くだけた会話で
（ブライアンはセックスアピールがありません）
Brian ◎ Ⓐ turns me off.
　　　 ◎ Ⓑ doesn't turn me on.
　　　 ○ Ⓒ isn't sexy.
　　　 × Ⓓ isn't hot.
　●かしこまって述べるとき
（ブライアンはセックスアピールがありません）
◎ Ⓐ Brian isn't physically attractive to me.
◎ Ⓑ Brian isn't sexually attractive to me.
◎ Ⓒ I'm not physically attracted to Brian.
◎ Ⓓ I'm not sexually attracted to Brian.
○ Ⓔ Brian doesn't appeal to me physically [sexually].
○ Ⓕ Brian doesn't have sexual appeal to me.
[注意] 友人同士の会話でもⒶ〜Ⓕがときどき使われることがある。

4 「(人が) やせている」
（彼はやせている）
He's ◎ Ⓐ thin.
　　　◎ Ⓑ lean.
[注意] Ⓐは普通，病気などでやせているときに使われている。ⒷはⒶほどやせていない。体質的に皮下脂肪が少なくやせているときに使われている。

5 「やせこけている」
(a) 一般的に述べる場合
（ポールはやせこけています）
Paul's ◎ Ⓐ all [just] skin and bones.
　　　 ◎ Ⓑ skinny [scrawny].
　　　 △ Ⓒ a walking [living] skeleton.
　　　 △ Ⓓ a bag of bones.
　　　 × Ⓔ worn to skeleton [a shadow].
　　　 × Ⓕ cadaverous.
　　　 × Ⓖ a rackabones [a rack of bones, an anatomy].
[注意] ⒺⒻⒼが辞典に出ているが使われていない。

(b) **背が高くてやせていることを強調する場合**
（ポールはやせこけています）
Paul's ◎ Ⓐ a bean pole.
　　　　◎ Ⓑ lanky.
　　　　○ Ⓒ a string bean.
　　　　○ Ⓓ gangly.
[注意] 背の高い順はⒶ, Ⓑ, Ⓒ, Ⓓ。

6 「（寝不足で）やつれた」
（リサは寝不足でやつれた顔をしていました）
Lisa looked ☆ Ⓐ worn-out from lack of sleep.
　　　　　　☆ Ⓑ exhausted [really tired] ...
　　　　　　◎ Ⓒ wiped out ...
　　　　　　△ Ⓓ gaunt [worn, haggard] ...
　　　　　　× Ⓔ wasted [emaciated] ...

7 「太っている」
(a) **客観的に述べる場合**
（主人は体重がオーバーなんです）
◎ My husband's overweight [obese].

(b) **主観的に述べる場合**
　●男性
（次男は太っているんです）
My second son's ☆ Ⓐ heavy [big, flabby].
　　　　　　　　◎ Ⓑ large [stout].
　　　　　　　　○ Ⓒ portly.

　●女性
（下から2番目の娘は太っているんです）
My second youngest daughter's ☆ Ⓐ heavy [big, flabby].
　　　　　　　　　　　　　　　◎ Ⓑ large.
　　　　　　　　　　　　　　　△ Ⓒ plump [beerbellied].
[注意] 辞典に She's stout [portly, corn-fed]. が出ているが使われていない。

8 「太り気味」

(キャスィーは太り気味なんです)
Cathy's ☆ Ⓐ a little heavy [big].
　　　　◎ Ⓑ a kind of heavy [big].
　　　　◎ Ⓒ on the heavy side.
　　　　○ Ⓓ a little large.
　　　　○ Ⓔ kind of large.
　　　　○ Ⓕ somewhat heavy [large].
　　　　△ Ⓖ sort of big [heavy].

9 「でぶ」
(ベッキーはでぶなんです)
Becky's ☆ Ⓐ fat.
　　　　◎ Ⓑ fast-ass.
　　　　◎ Ⓒ as big as a house.
　　　　◎ Ⓓ chubby [chunky].
　　　　○ Ⓔ pudgy [a fatso, a cow, as big as a whale [an elephant]].
　　　　△ Ⓕ a tab of lard [as big as a cow].

[注意] (1) chubby, chunky, pudgy は20歳以下の人を述べるときに普通使われている。
(2) Ⓑが1番批判しているニュアンスがある。ⒶとⒺの fatso が2番，残りはほぼ同じ。

10 「体重を減らす」
(a) 一般的に述べるとき
(医師：あなたは体重を減らしたほうがいいですよ)
Doctor: You'd better ☆ Ⓐ lose weight.
　　　　　　　　　　◎ Ⓑ slim down.
　　　　　　　　　　◎ Ⓒ take some of the weight off.
　　　　　　　　　　◎ Ⓓ be on a diet.
　　　　　　　　　　△ Ⓔ take off weight.

[注意] (1) 辞典に decrease [reduce] weight が出ているが使われていない。
(2) Ⓓは原義は「規定食を食べる」という意味であったが，最近「体重を減らす」の意味でよく使われるようになった。

(b) 下腹部のぜい肉を頭に置いて述べるとき
　　● 男性

[82]

第7章　容姿に関する表現

(私は体重を減らさなければならないんです)
　　○ I have to get rid of my love handles [my beer belly, my pot belly, my belly, my space tire, my love handle].
● 女性
(私は体重を減らさなければならないんです)
I have to get rid of
　　○ Ⓐ my love handles.
　　△ Ⓑ my belly [my roll, my beer belly, my pot belly].

11 「太らないように気をつけている」
(私は太らないように気をつけています)
I'm ☆ Ⓐ watching my weight.
　　◎ Ⓑ watching my waistline.
　　◎ Ⓒ trying not to gain weight.
　　◎ Ⓓ careful about my weight.
　　△ Ⓔ careful not to gain weight.

12 「リバウンドする」
(a)　リバウンドした程度に言及しない場合
(リンダは体重がリバウンドしてしまったんです)
Linda's ◎ Ⓐ gained the weight back.
　　　　 ◎ Ⓑ put the weight back on.
　　　　 △ Ⓒ regained the weight.
　　　　 × Ⓓ rebounded the weight.
[注意] rebound は体重には使えない。失意, 失敗, 病気などから「立ち直る」の意味ではよく使われている。

(b)　少し体重が増えた場合
(ナンシーは少しリバウンドしてしまったんです)
Nancy's ◎ Ⓐ gained some weight back.
　　　　 ◎ Ⓑ gained a little weight back.
　　　　 ◎ Ⓒ put a little weight back on.
　　　　 ○ Ⓓ put a little weight back.
　　　　 △ Ⓔ put back on a little weight.

(c)　完全に元に戻ってしまった場合
(メアリーは体重がリバウンドしてしまったんです)

Mary's ◎ Ⓐ gained all the weight back.
　　　 ◎ Ⓑ put all the weight back on.
　　　 ◎ Ⓒ put weight back on.
　　　 ○ Ⓓ gained the weight completely.
　　　 ○ Ⓔ regained all the weight back.

13 「(顔が) 可愛い」

(a)　息子
　　（彼女には可愛い息子さんがいるんです）
　　She has ☆ Ⓐ a cute little son.
　　　　　 ☆ Ⓑ a sweet little son.
　　　　　 ◎ Ⓒ an adorable little son.

(b)　娘
　　（リンダには可愛い娘がいるんです）
　　Linda has ☆ Ⓐ a cute little girl.
　　　　　　 ◎ Ⓑ an adorable girl.
　　　　　　 ◎ Ⓒ a pretty little girl.
　　　　　　 ○ Ⓓ a pretty little thing.
［注意］(1) 可愛さの点ではⒷが1番，ⒸⒹが2番，Ⓐが3番。
(2) ⒷⒹは5, 6歳，ⒶⒸは8歳位までの子供に使われている。

(c)　動物
　　（ナンシーは可愛い犬を飼っています）
　　Nancy has ☆ Ⓐ a cute dog.
　　　　　　 ◎ Ⓑ an adorable dog.
　　　　　　 ○ Ⓒ a beautiful dog.
　　　　　　 △ Ⓓ a pretty dog.
　　　　　　 × Ⓔ a good-looking dog.

14 「(笑顔が) 可愛い」

　　（ボブの笑顔は可愛いわね）
　　Bob has ☆ Ⓐ a cute smile.
　　　　　 ☆ Ⓑ an adorable smile.
　　　　　 ◎ Ⓒ a sweet smile.
［注意］ボブが幼い男の子ならば誰でも「可愛い」と表現する。30歳位ならば，70歳位の女性の間でよく使われている。

第 7 章　容姿に関する表現

15 「可愛いくてしようがない」
（あの男の子は可愛いくてしようがないわね）
That boy's so ☆ Ⓐ cute I just love him.
　　　　　　　☆ Ⓑ sweet ...
　　　　　　　◎ Ⓒ adorable ...

16 「10人並み」
（今度の秘書は美人なの）
Is the new secretary beautiful?
（いや，10人並みだよ）
No, ◎ Ⓐ she's OK.
　　◎ Ⓑ she's just average.
　　◎ Ⓒ she's all right.
　　◎ Ⓓ she isn't so bad.
　　○ Ⓔ she's so so.
　　▽ Ⓕ she's mediocre.
　　× Ⓖ she's on (an) average.

17 「美人」
(a)　普通に述べる場合
（ナンシーは美人です）
Nancy's ☆ Ⓐ beautiful ［gorgeous, good-looking］.
　　　　◎ Ⓑ a knockout.
　　　　◎ Ⓒ lovely ［pretty］.
　　　　○ Ⓓ stunner.
［注意］「美人」の程度は knockout, gorgeous が 1 番, stunner が 2 番。

(b)　「すごい美人」と述べる場合
（ナンシーはすごい美人です）
Nancy's ☆ Ⓐ really beautiful.
　　　　◎ Ⓑ very beautiful.
　　　　◎ Ⓒ a real knockout ［stunner］.
　　　　◎ Ⓓ a real beauty.
　　　　◎ Ⓔ really ［very］ gorgeous.
　　　　○ Ⓕ a stunning beauty.
［注意］多くの辞典に a beauty（美人）と出ているが，ⒹⒻのように a ＋形容

詞＋beauty で使う。

(c) 「セクシー」であるという意味の「すごい美人」
　　（ナンシーはすごい美人です）
　　Nancy's ◎ Ⓐ really hot.
　　　　　　△ Ⓑ a real babe.
　　　　　　▽ Ⓒ a doll.

18 「いい男」
(a) 身体全体の容姿の場合
　　●普通に述べるとき
　　（ロジャーはいい男です）
　　Roger's ◎ Ⓐ good-looking.
　　　　　　△ Ⓑ a hunk ［a babe］.
　　●強調して述べるとき
　　（ロジャーはすごくいい男です）
　　Roger's ◎ Ⓐ gorgeous.
　　　　　　◎ Ⓑ really good-looking.

(b) 顔の場合
　　●普通に述べるとき
　　（ロジャーはいい男です）
　　◎ Roger's handsome.
　　●強調して述べるとき
　　（ロジャーはすごくいい男です）
　　Roger's ◎ Ⓐ really handsome.
　　　　　　○ Ⓑ very handsome.
　　●ずっと年上の女性が述べるとき
　　（ロジャーはいい男です）
　　◎ Roger's cute.
　　［注意］60歳以上の女性なら40歳位の男性にも使われている。

(c) セクシーだというニュアンスの場合
　　（ロジャーはいい男です）
　　Roger's ☆ Ⓐ hot.
　　　　　　◎ Ⓑ sexy.
　　　　　　○ Ⓒ a stud ［a babe］.

第 7 章　容姿に関する表現

△ ⓓ foxy [a fox].

19「つやつやした髪」
(彼女の髪はつやつやしています)
☆ ⓐ Her hair looks healthy.
☆ ⓑ She has healthy hair.
◎ ⓒ Her hair looks good.
◎ ⓓ She has good hair.
[注意] ⓒⓓは「ヘアスタイルがいい」という意味にもよく使われている。どちらであるかは話の前後から判断する。

20「しわ」
(ナンシーの顔はしわだらけです)
☆ ⓐ Nancy has a lot of wrinkles on her face.
◎ ⓑ Nancy's face is very wrinkled.
◎ ⓒ Nancy's face has a lot of wrinkles.
○ ⓓ Nancy's face has a lot of lines.
△ ⓔ Nancy has a lot of lines on her face.

21「日焼けする」
(a)　普通に日焼けしている場合
(ディックは日焼けしています)
◎ ⓐ Dick's tan.
◎ ⓑ Dick has a tan.
◎ ⓒ Dick has a suntan.
○ ⓓ Dick's suntanned.
○ ⓔ Dick's tanned.
× ⓕ Dick's sunburned.
[注意] (1) sunburnt, sunbrowned が辞典に出ているが使われていない。
(2) ⓕは「普通に日焼けしている」という意味では使われない。(c)を参照のこと。

(b)　非常に日焼けしている場合
(ディックはすごく日焼けしています)
◎ ⓐ Dick's real tan.
◎ ⓑ Dick's very tan.
◎ ⓒ Dick has a dark tan.

　　　　◯ Ⓓ Dick has a deep tan.

(c) 炎症を起こしている場合
　　（ディックは日焼けして皮膚が赤くなっている）
　　Dick's ◎ Ⓐ deeply sunburned.
　　　　　 ◎ Ⓑ seriously sunburned.
　　　　　 ◎ Ⓒ badly sunburned.

22 「肌が白い」
(a) 白人
　　（アイリーンは肌が白いです）
　　　◎ Ⓐ Eileen's fair-skinned [light-skinned].
　　　◎ Ⓑ Eileen has white [fair, light] skin.
　　　◎ Ⓒ Eileen has a fair [light] complexion.
　　　▽ Ⓓ Eileen has a white complexion.
　　　▽ Ⓔ Eileen's fair complected [complexioned].
　　　▽ Ⓕ Eileen's white-skinned.
　　　［注意］ⒹⒺⒻが辞典に出ているがまれ。

(b) 非白人
　　（京子は肌が白いんです）
　　　◎ Ⓐ Kyoko has light skin.
　　　◎ Ⓑ Kyoko's light-skinned.
　　　◎ Ⓒ Kyoko has a light [fair] complexion.
　　　△ Ⓓ Kyoko's light-complected.

23 「肌が黒い」
(a) 話し手が白人の場合
　　（彼女は肌が黒いんです）
　　　☆ Ⓐ She has dark skin.
　　　◎ Ⓑ She has a dark complexion.
　　　◯ Ⓒ She's dark-skinned.
　　　△ Ⓓ She's dark-complected.

(b) 話し手が非白人の場合
　　（彼女は肌が黒いんです）
　　　☆ Ⓐ She has dark skin.

◎ Ⓑ She's dark-skinned.
○ Ⓒ She has a dark complexion.
△ Ⓓ She's dark-complected.

24 「肌がきれいです」

(a) 顔
(リンダの肌はきれいですね)
Linda has ◎ Ⓐ smooth skin.
　　　　　◎ Ⓑ beautiful skin.

(b) 顔以外のとき
(リンダの肌はきれいですね)
Linda has ◎ Ⓐ smooth skin.
　　　　　◎ Ⓑ beautiful skin.

25 「つやつやした肌」

(彼女の肌はつやつやしていますね)
☆ Ⓐ She has good skin.
◎ Ⓑ She has healthy skin.
◎ Ⓒ Her skin looks healthy.
△ Ⓓ She has shy skin.
[注意] 辞典に sleek [slick, glossy, bright] skin, be shiny-faced が出ているが使われていない。

26 「肌が荒れている」

(リンダの肌はとても荒れているわね)
Linda has ◎ Ⓐ rough skin.
　　　　　× Ⓑ a rough skin.
[注意] 辞典にⒷが出ているが使われていない。

27 「目」

(a) 大きい目
(リンダの目は大きいです)
◎ Ⓐ Linda has big eyes.
△ Ⓑ Linda's eyes're big.

(b) 優しい目

（ビルは優しい目をしています）
　　　Bill has ◎ Ⓐ kind eyes.
　　　　　　　○ Ⓑ sweet eyes.
　　　［注意］辞典に have soft［tender］eyes が出ているが使われていない。

(c)　怖い目
　　　（ティムは怖い目をしています）
　　　Tim has ◎ Ⓐ menacing eyes.
　　　　　　　○ Ⓑ threatening eyes.

28 「まつ毛」
(a)　「きれいです」と述べる場合
　　　（彼女はまつ毛がきれいです）
　　　She has ☆ Ⓐ long, thick eyelashes.
　　　　　　　◎ Ⓑ long, thick lashes.
　　　　　　　◎ Ⓒ beautiful eyelashes.
　　　［注意］(1) 辞典に have beautiful lashes［winkers］が出ているが使われていない。
　　　　　　(2) A long and thick eyelash と and を使えない。

(b)　「長い」と述べる場合
　　　（彼女のまつ毛は長いんです）
　　　☆ Ⓐ She has long eyelashes.
　　　◎ Ⓑ Her eyelashes're long.
　　　○ Ⓒ Her lashes're long.
　　　○ Ⓓ She has long lashes.
　　　［注意］辞典に winkers が出ているが使われていない。

29 「ひげ」
(a)　本物のひげ
　　　（ジェフはひげをはやしている）
　　　Jeff ◎ Ⓐ has a mustache.
　　　　　× Ⓑ wears［is wearing］a mustache.
　　　　　× Ⓒ has on a mustache.
　　　［注意］ⒷⒸは辞典に出ているが使われていない。

(b)　つけひげ

（ジェフはつけひげをつけている）
　　◎ Ⓐ Jeff's wearing a fake mustache.
　　◎ Ⓑ Jeff has on a fake mustache.
　　◎ Ⓒ Jeff wears a fake mustache.

30 「鼻がかっこいい」
　　（ナンシーの鼻はかっこいいです）
　　Nancy has ☆ Ⓐ a nice nose.
　　　　　　　 ◎ Ⓑ a beautiful nose.
　　　　　　　 ◎ Ⓒ a great nose.
　　　　　　　 ○ Ⓓ a terrific nose.
　　[注意] (1) 辞典に have a well-cut nose, have a shapely nose が出ているが使われていない。
　　　　　(2) Ⓑは男性に使うと使用頻度は下がる。

31 「鼻が上を向いている」
　　（彼女の鼻は上を向いています）
　　◎ Ⓐ She has an upturned nose.
　　○ Ⓑ Her nose is turned up.
　　× Ⓒ She has a turned-up nose.
　　× Ⓓ Her nose is upturned.
　　[注意] 辞典にⒸⒹが出ているが使われていない。

32 「鼻があぐらをかいている」
　　（彼女は鼻があぐらをかいています）
　　☆ Ⓐ She has a wide, flat nose.
　　◎ Ⓑ She has a broad, flat nose.
　　◎ Ⓒ She has a broad and flat nose.
　　○ Ⓓ Her nose is broad and flat.

33 「美容整形手術」
(a) **目・鼻などの形を整える手術**
　　●鼻
　　（リンダは鼻の美容整形手術をしたんです）
　　Linda had [got] ◎ Ⓐ a nose job.
　　　　　　　　　 ○ Ⓑ her nose done.
　　●あご

（キャロルはあごの美容整形手術をしたんです）
　　　Carol had［got］◎ Ⓐ a chin job.
　　　　　　　　　　　○ Ⓑ her chin done.
　　●胸
　　　（キャスィーは胸の美容整形手術をしたんです）
　　　Cathy had［got］◎ Ⓐ a boob job.
　　　　　　　　　　　◎ Ⓑ a breast job.
　　　　　　　　　　　○ Ⓒ her breasts done.
　　　　　　　　　　　○ Ⓓ her boobs done.
　　●目
　　　（ナンシーは目の美容整形手術をしたんです）
　　　Nancy had［got］◎ Ⓐ her eyes done.
　　　　　　　　　　　○ Ⓑ an eye job.

(b)　**しわ取りの手術**
　　　（スィンディーは顔のしわ取りの美容整形手術をしたんです）
　　　Cindy had［got］◎ Ⓐ a face-lift.
　　　　　　　　　　　○ Ⓑ her face done.

34 「油で汚れた」
(a)　**手**
　　　（彼は車の修理工なので手はいつも油で汚れているんです）
　　　His hands're always ◎ Ⓐ greasy because he's a car mechanic.
　　　　　　　　　　　　× Ⓑ oily ...

(b)　**髪の毛**
　　　（彼の髪の毛はいつも油で汚れているように見える）
　　　His hair always looks ◎ Ⓐ greasy.
　　　　　　　　　　　　　○ Ⓑ oily.

35 「（人が）似ている」
(a)　**容姿**
　　　（ブライアンは母親にとてもよく似ています）
　　　Brian ☆ Ⓐ looks a lot［just］like his mother.
　　　　　　☆ Ⓑ really looks like his mother.
　　　　　　☆ Ⓒ looks like his mother a lot.
　　　　　　◎ Ⓓ really takes after his mother.

◎ Ⓔ takes after his mother a lot.
○ Ⓕ looks a great deal like his mother.
○ Ⓖ looks like his mother a great deal.
○ Ⓗ really resembles his mother.
○ Ⓘ resembles his mother a lot.
○ Ⓙ has a strong [striking] resemblance to his mother.
○ Ⓚ bears a strong resemblance to his mother.

(b) **性格**
(ブライアンは母親にとてもよく似ています)
◎ Ⓐ Brian really takes after his mother.
◎ Ⓑ Brian takes after his mother a lot.
◎ Ⓒ Brian's a lot [just] like his mother.
○ Ⓓ Brian's a great deal [very much] like his mother.
○ Ⓔ Brian favors his mother a lot.
○ Ⓕ Brian really favors his mother.
[注意] (1) ⒶⒷは容姿が似ていることを言うのにも使うことができる。
(2) ⒺⒻは「ブライアンはお母さんのほうがとても好きなんです」の意味でもよく使われている

(c) **瓜ふたつ**
(ブライアンは母親に瓜ふたつです)
Brian's ◎ Ⓐ a carbon copy of his mother.
　　　　◎ Ⓑ the spitting [the exact] image of his mother.
　　　　△ Ⓒ the perfect likeness [image] of his mother.
　　　　△ Ⓓ the very picture of his mother.
　　　　△ Ⓔ his mother's double.
[注意] a chip off [of] the old block が辞典に出ているが父親には使われているが母親には使われていない。

第8章

服装に関する表現

1 「似合う」
(a) **物が主語の場合**

●強調しないで述べるとき
(そのグリーンのスーツはあなたに似合います)

That green suit ☆ Ⓐ looks good on you.
　　　　　　　　◎ Ⓑ fits [suits] you.
　　　　　　　　○ Ⓒ does something for you.
　　　　　　　　○ Ⓓ becomes you.
　　　　　　　　△ Ⓔ is becoming on you.
　　　　　　　　▽ Ⓕ is becoming to you.
　　　　　　　　× Ⓖ fits [sits] well on you.

[注意] Ⓖが辞典に出ているのが使われていない。

●強い形容詞または名詞を使って強調するとき
(そのグリーンのスーツはあなたにすごく似合いますよ)

That green suit looks ☆ Ⓐ great on you.
　　　　　　　　　　　◎ Ⓑ terrific [wonderful] on you.
　　　　　　　　　　　◎ Ⓒ fantastic [incredible, amazing] on you.
　　　　　　　　　　　○ Ⓓ super on you.
　　　　　　　　　　　△ Ⓔ the bomb on you.
　　　　　　　　　　　△ Ⓕ superb on you.
　　　　　　　　　　　△ Ⓖ marvelous on you.

[注意] (1) ほめている強さはⒸが1番，ⒷⒺⒼが2番，ⒶⒹⒻは3番。
(2) Ⓔは若年層，特に20歳前後の人たちの間では非常によく使われている。

[94]

●形容詞を強調して述べるとき
(そのグリーンのスーツはあなたにすごく似合いますよ)
That green suit looks ☆ Ⓐ really great on you.
　　　　　　　　　　　◎ Ⓑ really terrific [fantastic, incredible] on you.
　　　　　　　　　　　◎ Ⓒ really wonderful [amazing] on you.
　　　　　　　　　　　○ Ⓓ really super on you.
　　　　　　　　　　　△ Ⓔ really superb on you.

●動詞を強調して述べるとき
(そのグリーンのスーツはあなたにものすごく似合いますよ)
That green suit ☆ Ⓐ really looks great on you.
　　　　　　　　◎ Ⓑ really looks terrific [fantastic, incredible, wonderful, amazing] on you.
　　　　　　　　○ Ⓒ really looks super on you.
　　　　　　　　○ Ⓓ really suits [fits] on you.
　　　　　　　　○ Ⓔ really does something for you.
　　　　　　　　○ Ⓕ really becomes you.
　　　　　　　　△ Ⓖ really looks superb [the bomb] on you.
　　　　　　　　△ Ⓗ is really [very] becoming on you.
　　　　　　　　▽ Ⓘ is really [very] becoming to you.

(b) **人が主語の場合**
●in を使って言うとき
(マイクはそのブルーのスーツがものすごく似合いますよ)
Mike ◎ Ⓐ looks really great [terrific, fantastic, incredible, wonderful, amazing] in that blue suit.
　　　○ Ⓑ looks really good [nice] in ...
　　　△ Ⓒ really looks the bomb in ...
　　　△ Ⓓ looks really super [superb] in ...

●with を使って言うとき
(マイクはそのブルーのスーツがものすごく似合いますよ)
Mike ☆ Ⓐ looks really great with that blue suit on.
　　　◎ Ⓑ looks really terrific [fantastic, incredible, wonderful, amazing] with ...
　　　○ Ⓒ looks really good [nice] with ...
　　　△ Ⓓ really looks the bomb with ...
　　　△ Ⓔ looks really super [superb] with ...

2「色が合う」
(その紫色の上着は黒のスカートに合いますね)
That purple jacket ◎ Ⓐ goes (well) with the black skirt.
　　　　　　　　　　 ◎ Ⓑ works well [looks good] with the ...
　　　　　　　　　　 ◎ Ⓒ matches the ...
　　　　　　　　　　 ○ Ⓓ complements the ...
［注意］(1) 辞典に mix well with, fit well on, hormonize well with が出ているが使われていない。
(2) Ⓓは堅い響きがある。

3「コーディネート」
(a)「コーディネートされている」ことを述べるとき
(あなたの服はよくコーディネートされています)
◎ Ⓐ Your clothes're well-cordinated.
◎ Ⓑ Your outfit's well-cordinated.

(b)「コーディネートさせる」ことを述べるとき
(彼女は洋服をコーディネートさせるいいセンスを持っています)
She has a good sense of ◎ Ⓐ cordinating her clothes.
　　　　　　　　　　　　　　 ○ Ⓑ cordinating her outfit.
　　　　　　　　　　　　　　 ○ Ⓒ matching her clothes.
　　　　　　　　　　　　　　 △ Ⓓ matching her outfit.

4「ファッションのセンスがいい」
(リンダはファッションのセンスがいいです)
☆ Ⓐ Linda has good fashion sense.
◎ Ⓑ Linda has a good sense of fashion.
◎ Ⓒ Linda's stylish.
◎ Ⓓ Linda always has the latest look.
○ Ⓔ Linda's trendy.
△ Ⓕ Linda's fashionable.

5「着ている」
(a) 現在の状態
(素敵なスーツを着ていますね)
That's a nice suit ◎ Ⓐ you're wearing.

◎ ⓑ you have on.
[注意] (1) 辞典に you're in, you're dressed in が出ているが使われてもまれ。
(2) That に相当する日本語はないが「それは」の意味。

(b) 現在の状態として名詞を修飾している場合
(紫色の上着を着ている男の方はどなたですか)
Who's the gentleman ☆ Ⓐ with the purple jacket on?
　　　　　　　　　　☆ Ⓑ in the purple jacket on?
　　　　　　　　　　◎ Ⓒ with the purple jacket?
　　　　　　　　　　◎ Ⓓ that's wearing the purple jacket?
　　　　　　　　　　◎ Ⓔ that has on the purple jacket?
　　　　　　　　　　◎ Ⓕ wearing the purple jacket?
　　　　　　　　　　◎ Ⓖ that has the purple jacket on?
　　　　　　　　　　◎ Ⓗ dressed in the purple jacket?
　　　　　　　　　　× Ⓘ having the purple jacket on?

(c) 過去の一時的状態
(ボブは昨日のパーティーでグレーのスーツを着ていました)
Bob ◎ Ⓐ was wearing a gray suit at the party yesterday.
　　 ◎ Ⓑ had on a gray suit ...
　　 ◎ Ⓒ had a gray suit on ...
　　 ◎ Ⓓ was dressed in a gray suit ...
　　 ◎ Ⓔ was in a gray suit ...
　　 ◎ Ⓕ wore a gray suit ...

(d) 過去の習慣的内容を表す文で **every day** がある場合
(彼女は結婚する前毎日違ったドレスを着ていました)
She ☆ Ⓐ wore a different dress every day before she got married.
　　 ◎ Ⓑ had on ...
　　 ○ Ⓒ was in ...
　　 △ Ⓓ was wearing ...
　　 △ Ⓔ was dressed in ...

(e) 過去の習慣的内容として述べるとき
(当時は日本人だけでなくアメリカ人も非常に地味な服を着ていました)
Back then not only Japanese people but also Americans

◎ Ⓐ wore really conservative clothes.
○ Ⓑ were wearing ...
○ Ⓒ had ...
△ Ⓓ were dressed in ...
△ Ⓔ were in ...
▽ Ⓕ had on ...

6 「着飾っている」
(彼女はパーティーで黄色いドレスに黄色い帽子で着飾っていました)
She was ☆ Ⓐ really dressed up in a yellow dress with a yellow hat
　　　　　◎ Ⓑ decked out in ...
at the party.

7 「趣味に合わない」
(その色は私の趣味に合いません)
☆ Ⓐ That isn't my color.
☆ Ⓑ That color doesn't look good on me.
◎ Ⓒ I don't look good in that color.
○ Ⓓ That color isn't for me.
○ Ⓔ That color doesn't look attractive on me.

8 「流行する」
(a) 現在（流行しています）
(ブルーが今年は流行しています)
Blue's ☆ Ⓐ "in" this year.
　　　　◎ Ⓑ hot [popular, fashionable, in fashion] ...
　　　　○ Ⓒ in style ...
　　　　△ Ⓓ in vogue ...
　　　　△ Ⓔ the craze ...

(b) 未来（流行するでしょう）
(ブルーが来年は流行するでしょう)
Blue'll ☆ Ⓐ be "in" next year.
　　　　☆ Ⓑ be popular ...
　　　　◎ Ⓒ be in style ...
　　　　◎ Ⓓ come in style ...
　　　　◎ Ⓔ be hot ...

第 8 章　服装に関する表現

　　　◎ Ⓕ in fashion ...
　　　○ Ⓖ become popular ...
　　　○ Ⓗ come into [in] fashion [vogue] ...
　　　○ Ⓘ be the fad [the craze] ...

(c)　**大流行している**
　　（ブルーが今大流行しています）
　　Blue's ◎ Ⓐ really popular now.
　　　　　○ Ⓑ all the rage now.
　　[注意] all the fashion [the style, the fad, the craze, the vogue] が辞典に出ているが使われていない。

9 「流行を追う」
　　（彼女は非常に流行を追っています）
　　☆ Ⓐ She really follows (the) current [latest] fashions [styles, trends].
　　◎ Ⓑ She really follows (the) fashions [styles, trends].
　　◎ Ⓒ She really chases after the current [latest].
　　◎ Ⓓ She's really trendy.
　　△ Ⓔ She's fashion-oriented [fashion-minded].
　　△ Ⓕ She's trend-oriented [style-oriented].

10 「流行の先端をいく」
　　（彼女は流行の先端をいっています）
　　She's ☆ Ⓐ a trendsetter.
　　　　　☆ Ⓑ setting the latest [current] fashions [styles, trends].
　　　　　◎ Ⓒ a fashionsetter.
　　　　　○ Ⓓ setting the fashions [styles, trends].

11 「流行に遅れない」
　　（私は流行に遅れたくないんです）
　　I want to keep up with ☆ Ⓐ the current fashions [styles].
　　　　　　　　　　　　　 ◎ Ⓑ the latest fashions [styles].
　　　　　　　　　　　　　 ○ Ⓒ the current fads.
　　　　　　　　　　　　　 ○ Ⓓ the latest fads.
　　[注意] keep up with と並べて keep pace with を紹介している辞典があるが使われていない。

12「流行に振りまわされている」
　　（彼女は流行に振りまわされています）
　　She's ☆ Ⓐ a slave to the latest fashions.
　　　　　◎ Ⓑ a slave to the current fashions.
　　　　　○ Ⓒ at the mercy of the latest fashions.
　　　　　△ Ⓓ swayed by the latest fashions.

13「オーダーメイドの」
　　（このスーツはオーダーメイドです）
　　This is ☆ Ⓐ a custom-made suit.
　　　　　　◎ Ⓑ a tailor-made suit.
　　　　　　○ Ⓒ a custom-tailored suit.
　　　　　　○ Ⓓ a made-to-order suit.
　　　　　　○ Ⓔ a suit made-to-order.
　　　　　　△ Ⓕ a suit tailor-made ［custom-made］.
　　［注意］辞典に order-made suit, custom suit, made-to-measure suit, suit made-to-measure が出ているが使われていない。

14「イージーオーダーの」
　　（これはイージーオーダーのスーツです）
　　This is × Ⓐ a semi-order-made suit.
　　　　　　× Ⓑ a semi-custom-made suit.
　　　　　　× Ⓒ a semi-tailored suit.
　　　　　　× Ⓓ a semi-tailor-made suit.
　　　　　　× Ⓔ a suit made to order without a fitting.
　　　　　　× Ⓕ a suit tailor-made without a fitting.
　　　　　　× Ⓖ a suit custom-made without a fitting.
　　　　　　× Ⓗ a suit order-made without a fitting.
　　［注意］辞典にⒶ～Ⓗが出ているがアメリカではイージーオーダーがないので使われていない。

15「既製の」
　　（このスーツは既製品です）
　　☆ Ⓐ This suit's off-the-rack.
　　◎ Ⓑ This is off-the-rack suit.
　　○ Ⓒ This is a ready-made suit.

[注意] 辞典に This suit's ready to wear. が出ているが使われていない。

16 「胸のあいた」
(彼女は胸のあいたドレスをパーティーで着ていました)
She was wearing ☆ Ⓐ a low cut dress at the party.
　　　　　　　　◯ Ⓑ a dress with a low neckline.
　　　　　　　　△ Ⓒ a dress with a plunging neckline.

17 「ロングドレス」
(私はパーティーに着ていくロングドレスを買いたいんです)
I want to buy ☆ Ⓐ a long dress to wear to the party.
　　　　　　　◎ Ⓑ an evening dress ...

18 「長袖のシャツ」
(私は長袖のシャツを買いたいんです)
I want to buy ☆ Ⓐ a long-sleeved shirt.
　　　　　　　◎ Ⓑ a shirt with long sleeves.
　　　　　　　◯ Ⓒ a shirt that has long sleeves.

19 「サイズ」
(a) 2まわり大きいと述べる場合
　　(デパートでの客：このスーツは2まわり大きいのはありますか)
　　☆ Ⓐ Do you have this suit in two sizes larger?
　　◎ Ⓑ Is this suit available in two sizes larger?

(b) サイズを述べる場合
　　(デパートでの客：このスーツは14サイズはありますか)
　　☆ Ⓐ Do you have this suit in size 14?
　　◎ Ⓑ Do you have this suit in 14?
　　△ Ⓒ Is this suit available in 14?

20 「クツのサイズ」
(あなたのクツのサイズはいくつですか)
☆ Ⓐ What size shoe do you wear?
◎ Ⓑ What's your shoesize?
◯ Ⓒ What size shoes do you wear?
◯ Ⓓ What size do you take in shoes?

21 「ぴったり」
(a) **サイズを述べるとき**

(店員：そのグリーンのドレスはお客様にぴったりですね)

That green dress ☆ Ⓐ fits you perfect [perfectly].
　　　　　　　　◎ Ⓑ fits you like a glove.
　　　　　　　　◎ Ⓒ is a perfect fit.
　　　　　　　　◎ Ⓓ is exactly the right size for you.
　　　　　　　　○ Ⓔ fits you exactly.
　　　　　　　　○ Ⓕ is perfectly-fitting on you.
　　　　　　　　△ Ⓖ fits you to a T.

［注意］(1) 辞典に fits you like a skin, a perfect to you が出ているが使われていない。

(2) Ⓓ以外のⒶⒷⒸⒺⒻⒼは約75％はサイズに言及しているが、約25％は「似合っている」というニュアンスもある。

(b) **似合うと述べたいとき**

(店員：そのグリーンのドレスはお客様にぴったりです)

☆ Ⓐ That green dress looks perfect on you.
◎ Ⓑ That green dress matches you perfect.
◎ Ⓒ That green dress fits [suits] you perfect.
◎ Ⓓ You look perfect in that green dress.

［注意］(1) ⒷⒸの perfect は perfectly が正しく、またよく使われているが会話では perfect のほうがよく使われている。

(2) この会話が友人同士ならⒸの suit は堅くなるので使用頻度は下がる。

22 「だぶだぶした」
(a) **ズボン**

(これらのズボンは全部私にはだぶだぶです)

All of these pants're ◎ Ⓐ baggy on me.
　　　　　　　　　　◎ Ⓑ loose on me.

(b) **スーツ・上着**

(このスーツは私にはだぶだぶです)

This suit's ◎ Ⓐ too big for me.
　　　　　　○ Ⓑ too large for me.
　　　　　　○ Ⓒ too loose for me.

第8章　服装に関する表現

23 「詰める」
(袖を詰めてくれますか)
Would you ☆ Ⓐ hem my sleeves?
　　　　　◎ Ⓑ shorten my sleeves?
　　　　　○ Ⓒ take up my sleeves?
　　　　　○ Ⓓ take my sleeves up?

24 「取れかかっている」
(あなたの上着のボタンが取れかかっている)
A button on your jacket's ◎ Ⓐ loose.
　　　　　　　　　　　　　◎ Ⓑ coming [falling] off.
　　　　　　　　　　　　　◎ Ⓒ about to fall [come] off.
　　　　　　　　　　　　　△ Ⓓ just going to fall [come] off.

25 「長持ちする」
(あの生地は長持ちします)
That fabric ☆ Ⓐ lasts a long time.
　　　　　　◎ Ⓑ lasts long [for a long time].
　　　　　　◎ Ⓒ is durable.
　　　　　　○ Ⓓ is long-lasting.
　　　　　　○ Ⓔ wears well [stands up].
　　　　　　× Ⓕ stands a good deal of wear.
　　　　　　× Ⓖ keeps long.
［注意］辞典にⒻⒼが出ているのが使わていない。

26 「(生地が) すり切れる」
(この生地はたぶんすぐすり切れるでしょう)
This fabric'll ◎ Ⓐ very likely be worn out soon.
　　　　　　　◎ Ⓑ very likely wear out soon.
　　　　　　　× Ⓒ very likely wear soon.
　　　　　　　× Ⓓ very likely become threadbare [seedy] soon.
［注意］ⒸⒹが辞典に出ているが全く使われていない。

27 「しわ」
(a) **衣服**
(あなたの黄色いドレスはしわだらけです)

[103]

Your yellow ◎ Ⓐ dress has a lot of wrinkles.
　　　　　　◎ Ⓑ dress's really wrinkled.
　　　　　　◎ Ⓒ dress's very wrinkled.

(b) 生地
（その生地はしわになりやすいんです）
That fabric ◎ Ⓐ wrinkles [gets wrinkled] easily.
　　　　　　△ Ⓑ is easy to wrinkle [get wrinkled].

(c) 生地と折り目
（これらの生地は折りじわがつきやすいんです）
These fabrics ◎ Ⓐ crease easily.
　　　　　　　○ Ⓑ get creased easily.
　　　　　　　△ Ⓒ are easy to crease.

(d) 折り目
（ビル：ねえ，このズボンにアイロンをかけてくれるかい。折り目がはっきりしないんだ）
Bill: Honey, will you iron these pants?
　　　◎ Ⓐ The creases aren't sharp enough.
　　　× Ⓑ The lines aren't sharp enough.

28 「無地の」
（リンダは無地のドレスをパーティーで着ていました）
Linda was wearing ◎ Ⓐ a plain dress at the party.
　　　　　　　　　○ Ⓑ a solid color dress ...
　　　　　　　　　△ Ⓒ a solid colored dress ...
　　　　　　　　　△ Ⓓ a plain dress without a pattern ...
　　　　　　　　　× Ⓔ a unfigured dress ...
　　　　　　　　　× Ⓕ a dress of solid color ...
［注意］ⒺⒻが辞典に出ているが使われていない。

29 「水玉の」
(a) 普通に述べるとき
（彼女は水玉のドレスをパーティーで着ていました）
She was wearing ☆ Ⓐ a polka-dot dress at the party.
　　　　　　　　◎ Ⓑ a dress with polka dots ...

　　　　　　　　　　　　　　　　　　　　　第8章　服装に関する表現

　　　　　　　　○ ⓒ a polka-dotted dress ...

(b)　「大きな水玉の」と述べるとき
　　（彼女は大きな水玉のドレスをパーティーで着ていました）
　　She was wearing ☆ Ⓐ a dress with big polka dots at the party.
　　　　　　　　◎ Ⓑ a dress that has big polka dots ...
　　　　　　　　△ ⓒ a big-polka-dot dress ...
　　　　　　　　△ Ⓓ a big-polka-dotted dress ...

30 「花模様の」
(a)　サイズに言及しないとき
　　（リンダはパーティーで花模様のドレスを着ていました）
　　Linda was wearing ☆ Ⓐ a floral print dress at the party.
　　　　　　　　◎ Ⓑ a dress with a flower print ...
　　　　　　　　◎ ⓒ a dress with a flower pattern ...
　　　　　　　　○ Ⓓ a dress with a floral print ...
　　　　　　　　○ Ⓔ a flower-printed [flower-patterned]
　　　　　　　　　　　dress ...
　　　　　　　　△ Ⓕ a flower-designed dress ...
　　　　　　　　△ Ⓖ a dress with a flower design ...

(b)　サイズに言及するとき
　　（リンダは大きな花模様のドレスを着ていました）
　　Linda was wearing ☆ Ⓐ a dress with big flowers (on it).
　　　　　　　　◎ Ⓑ a dress with a big flower pattern.
　　　　　　　　○ ⓒ a dress with a big flower print.
　　　　　　　　○ Ⓓ a dress with a big floral pattern.
　　　　　　　　○ Ⓔ a dress with a big floral print.
　　　　　　　　△ Ⓕ a dress with a big floral design.

31 「しま模様の」
(a)　一般的に言う場合
　　（彼女はしま模様のドレスを着ていました）
　　She was wearing ☆ Ⓐ a striped dress.
　　　　　　　　☆ Ⓑ a dress that has stripes.
　　　　　　　　◎ ⓒ a dress with stripes.
　　　　　　　　△ Ⓓ a striped-patterned dress.

　　　　　△ Ⓔ a dress with a striped pattern.
　　　　　△ Ⓕ a dress that has a striped pattern.

(b)　太いしま模様の
　　（彼は太いしま模様のスーツを着ていました）
　　He was wearing a suit with ☆ Ⓐ wide stripes.
　　　　　　　　　　　　　　　◎ Ⓑ big stripes.
　　　　　　　　　　　　　　　◎ Ⓒ broad stripes.

(c)　細いしま模様の
　　（彼は細いしま模様のスーツを着ていました）
　　He was wearing a suit with ☆ Ⓐ narrow stripes.
　　　　　　　　　　　　　　　◎ Ⓑ thin stripes.
　　　　　　　　　　　　　　　○ Ⓒ small stripes.

32 「格子柄の」
（彼女は格子柄のウールの上着を着ていました）
◎ She was wearing a plaid wool jacket.
［注意］辞典に tartan が出ているが使われてもまれ。

33 「市様模様（碁盤縞）の」
（デイヴィッドは昨日市松模様のスーツを着ていました）
David was wearing ◎ Ⓐ a checked suit yesterday.
　　　　　　　　　○ Ⓑ a checkered suit ...
　　　　　　　　　○ Ⓒ a suit with a checked pattern ...
　　　　　　　　　○ Ⓓ a suit with checks ...
　　　　　　　　　△ Ⓔ a suit with a checkered pattern ...
［注意］辞典に chequered が出ているがアメリカ英語では使われていない。

34 「十字形模様の」
（リンダは十字形模様の上着を着ていました）
Linda was wearing ☆ Ⓐ a jacket with a criss-cross pattern.
　　　　　　　　　◎ Ⓑ a jacket with a criss-cross pattern on it.
　　　　　　　　　○ Ⓒ a criss-cross patterned jacket.

35 「長持ちする」
（このヘアカラーはあれより長持ちします）

第 8 章　服装に関する表現

This hair color ☆ Ⓐ lasts longer than that one.
　　　　　　　◎ Ⓑ lasts a longer time ...
　　　　　　　◎ Ⓒ stays in [holds up, holds up well, wears well] for a longer time ...
　　　　　　　○ Ⓓ is longer lasting ...
　　　　　　　△ Ⓔ keeps for a longer time ...

第9章

男女間に関する表現

1「どきどきする」
　（初めてデイヴィッドに紹介されたとき，私はどきどきしました）
　The first time I was introduced to David,
　　◎ Ⓐ my heart was racing.
　　◎ Ⓑ my heart was beating fast.
　　◎ Ⓒ my stomach was in knots.
　　◎ Ⓓ I couldn't breathe.
　　◎ Ⓔ I had butterflies in my stomach.
　　◎ Ⓕ she took my breath away.
　　○ Ⓖ my heart went pit-a-pat.
　　○ Ⓗ my jaw dropped.
　　△ Ⓘ I lost my breath.
　［注意］どきどきしていた度合いはⒽが1番強い。

2「愛している」
　（私はあなたを愛しています）
　　◎ Ⓐ I'm in love with you.
　　◎ Ⓑ I love you.
　［注意］Ⓐのほうが強い。

3「恋している」
　（彼はあなたにすごく恋していますよ）
　　☆ Ⓐ He's in love with you.
　　◎ Ⓑ He really has a crush on you.

◎ Ⓒ He's really got a crush on you.
　◎ Ⓓ He's really fallen in love with you.
　○ Ⓔ He's really fallen for you.
　○ Ⓕ He's really lost his heart to you.
［注意］ⒺはⒶⒷⒸⒹⒻより弱い響きがある。

4 「恋人」
(a) **女性**
　（彼女は私の恋人です）
　She's my ◎ Ⓐ girlfriend.
　　　　　 ○ Ⓑ girl.
　　　　　 △ Ⓒ sweetheart.
　　　　　 △ Ⓓ woman.
　［注意］(1) Ⓑは25歳以下の若い女性、Ⓓは30歳以上の女性に使われ、ⒶⒸは年齢に関係ない。従って老人の間でも非常によく使われている。
　(2) 辞典に my steady が出ているが使われていない。

(b) **男性**
　（ビルは私の恋人です）
　Bill's my ◎ Ⓐ boyfriend.
　　　　　 △ Ⓑ man.
　　　　　 △ Ⓒ sweetheart.
　［注意］Bill's my boy. は使われていない。

5 「夢中です」
(a) **10代の女性が一方的に夢中になっている場合**
　（バーバラは先生に夢中なんです）
　☆ Ⓐ Barbara has a crush on her teacher.
　☆ Ⓑ Barbara's infatuated with ...
　☆ Ⓒ Barbara's crazy about ...
　◎ Ⓓ Barbara's madly in love with ...
　○ Ⓔ Barbara's nuts about ...
　△ Ⓕ Barbara's mad for ［about］ ...
　△ Ⓖ Barbara's wild about ...
　× Ⓗ Barbara's dead gone on ...
　［注意］(1) Ⓐは10代の男の子が主語の場合には多少使われている。
　(2) ⒶⒷは「一方的な恋」。Ⓒ〜Ⓖは一方的、また両者が夢中になっている場合

にも使われている。

(b) 成人が一方的に夢中になっている場合
(リズはボブに夢中なんです)
☆ Ⓐ Liz's infatuated with Bob.
☆ Ⓑ Liz's crazy about ...
☆ Ⓒ Liz's totally [head over heels] in love with ...
◎ Ⓓ Liz's madly in love with ...
◎ Ⓔ Liz's nuts about ...
○ Ⓕ Liz's hooked on ...
△ Ⓖ Liz's mad for [about] ...
△ Ⓗ Liz's wild about ...
△ Ⓘ Liz has a crush on ...
△ Ⓙ Liz's pretty stuck on ...
× Ⓚ Liz's over (head and) ears in love with ...
× Ⓛ Liz's falling headlong in love with ...
× Ⓜ Liz has her head turned by ...
[注意] (1) 辞典にⓀⓁⓂが出ているが使われていない。
(2) Ⓐ以外は両面的な場合にも使われている。

(c) 年齢に関係なく両者が夢中になっている場合
(トムとナンシーはお互いに夢中なんです)
Tom and Nancy're ☆ Ⓐ crazy about each other.
　　　　　　　　　☆ Ⓑ head over heels in love with ...
　　　　　　　　　◎ Ⓒ totally in love with ...
　　　　　　　　　◎ Ⓓ nuts about ...
　　　　　　　　　○ Ⓔ madly in love with ...
　　　　　　　　　○ Ⓕ wild about [hooked on] ...
　　　　　　　　　△ Ⓖ mad for [about] ...

6 「熱い仲だ」
(2人はすごく熱い仲だ)
They're ☆ Ⓐ deeply in love with each other.
　　　　◎ Ⓑ madly in ...
　　　　○ Ⓒ really in ...
　　　　○ Ⓓ passionately in ...
　　　　○ Ⓔ sweetly on each other.

第9章　男女間に関する表現

［注意］Ⓓが1番強い。

7 「振られる」
(ボブはリンダに振られたんです)
- ◎ Ⓐ Linda dumped Bob.
- ○ Ⓑ Linda dropped Bob.
- ○ Ⓒ Bob was dumped by Linda.

［注意］(1) 辞典に jilt が「振られる」の意味で出ているが今は使われていない。
(2) 日本語は「振られる」と受身的に表現しているが英語ではⒶⒷのように能動的に表現する。

8 「気をもませる」
(ビル：いつ私たちは結婚できるのかい)
Bill: When can we get married?
(リンダ：分からないわ)
Linda: I don't know.
(ビル：気をもませないでくれよ)
Bill: Don't keep me ☆ Ⓐ hanging, please.
　　　　　　　　　☆ Ⓑ in suspense, ...
　　　　　　　　　◎ Ⓒ guessing, ...
　　　　　　　　　○ Ⓓ in limbo, ...
　　　　　　　　　△ Ⓔ on pins and needles, ...
　　　　　　　　　△ Ⓕ on the edge of my seat, ...
　　　　　　　　　× Ⓖ holding my breath, ...
　　　　　　　　　× Ⓗ breathless, ...
　　　　　　　　　× Ⓘ catching my breath, ...

［注意］(1) ⒼⒽⒾが辞典に出ているが使われていない。
(2) Ⓐが1番強い響きがあり，ⒷⒸⒹの順で下がる。

9 「大事にする」
(リンダと結婚したら，あなたを大事にしてくれるでしょう)
If you marry Linda, she'll ☆ Ⓐ take good care of you.
　　　　　　　　　　　　　◎ Ⓑ be really good to you.
　　　　　　　　　　　　　○ Ⓒ pamper you.
　　　　　　　　　　　　　○ Ⓓ treat you well.
　　　　　　　　　　　　　△ Ⓔ treat you like a king.

△ Ⓕ treat you like a prince.

[注意] Ⓐ〜Ⓓは男女を問わず使われているが，you が女性の場合はⒺは ... like a queen.，Ⓕは ... like a princess. を使う。しかし使用頻度はいずれも△。

10 「同棲する」
(a) 批判的に述べる場合
（リンダとビルは同棲しているんです）
Linda and Bill're ◎ Ⓐ shacking up.
　　　　　　　　　◎ Ⓑ shacking up together.
　　　　　　　　　○ Ⓒ living in sin.

(b) 客観的に述べる場合
（リンダとビルは同棲しています）
Linda and Bill're ◎ Ⓐ living together.
　　　　　　　　　▽ Ⓑ cohabiting.
　　　　　　　　　▽ Ⓒ cohabitating.
[注意] (1) 堅い文章ではⒷⒸはよく使われている。
(2) Ⓒは多くの辞典に出ていないが堅い文章では使われている。

11 「結婚する」
(a) 結婚する相手を述べる場合
（キャロルは億万長者と結婚するんです）
Carol's going to ◎ Ⓐ marry a billionaire.
　　　　　　　　△ Ⓑ get married to a billionaire.

(b) 結婚する相手を述べない場合
（ボブはいつ結婚するんですか）
When's Bob going to ☆ Ⓐ get married?
　　　　　　　　　　◎ Ⓑ be married?
　　　　　　　　　　△ Ⓒ marry [get hitched]?

12 「結婚記念日」
（今日は私たちの結婚記念日です）
◎ Ⓐ This is our (wedding) anniversary.
◎ Ⓑ Today is our (wedding) anniversary.
× Ⓒ Today is our marriage anniversary.

[注意] ⓒが辞典に出ているが使われていない。

13 「仲直りする」
(ナンシーとニールはまもなく仲直りするでしょう)
Nancy and Neil'll ◎ Ⓐ get back together [make up] soon.
　　　　　　　　 ◎ Ⓑ work things out soon.
　　　　　　　　 ○ ⓒ patch things up soon.
　　　　　　　　 △ Ⓓ reconcile soon.
　　　　　　　　 △ Ⓔ settle their differences soon.
　　　　　　　　 △ Ⓕ bury the hatchet soon.

[注意] Ⓕは1番深刻な響きがある。Ⓓが2番，ⒷⒸは3番。

14 「仲を取り持つ」
(私がサラとアンドルーの仲を取り持ったんです)
I ◎ Ⓐ got Sarah and Andrew together.
　◎ Ⓑ fixed [set] Sarah and Andrew up.
　◎ ⓒ played matchmaker for Sarah and Andrew.
　○ Ⓓ played the matchmaker for Sarah and Andrew.
　○ Ⓔ was the matchmaker for Sarah and Andrew.
　△ Ⓕ played cupid for Sarah and Andrew.
　△ Ⓖ hooked Sarah and Andrew up.

15 「結婚式」
(a) 式のとき
(私たちは結婚式の日を決めなければならないんです)
We have to set the date for our ◎ Ⓐ wedding.
　　　　　　　　　　　　　　　　△ Ⓑ wedding ceremony.
　　　　　　　　　　　　　　　　△ ⓒ wedding service.
　　　　　　　　　　　　　　　　× Ⓓ marriage ceremony [service].

[注意] Ⓓが辞典に出ているが使われていない。但し下記のように時間のことを言及するときはⓒは非常によく使われている。
We have to set the time for our wedding service.
(私たちは結婚式の時間を決めなければならないんです)

(b) 披露宴のとき
(彼らは私たちを披露宴に招待してくれました)
They invited us to their ◎ Ⓐ wedding reception.

　　　　　　　× Ⓑ wedding party.
[注意]（1）Ⓑが日本の英字紙によく出ているが使われていない。
（2）wedding party は「新郎，新婦，新郎の付添人（the best man），新婦の付添人（maid of honor），ときには新郎・新婦の両親も含めた人たち」の意味ではよく使われている。

16 「尻に敷かれている」
（彼は女房の尻に敷かれているんです）
☆ Ⓐ His wife wears the pants.
◎ Ⓑ His wife keeps her husband under her thumb.
◎ Ⓒ He's bossed around by his wife.
◎ Ⓓ He's a henpecked husband.
◎ Ⓔ His wife bosses him around.
◎ Ⓕ His wife dominates him.
◎ Ⓖ He's controlled by his wife.
◎ Ⓗ His wife orders him around.
△ Ⓘ He's a dominated husband.
△ Ⓙ He's dominated by his wife.
[注意] ⒷⒸⒹⒺⒻⒼⒽⒾⒿのほうがⒶよりずっと尻に敷かれているニュアンスが強い。

17 「家庭的」
（彼は家庭的な人［夫］です）
He's ☆ Ⓐ a family man.
　　　○ Ⓑ a family-oriented man［husband］.
　　　△ Ⓒ a family-minded husband.
[注意]（1）辞典に family husband, home-oriented husband が出ているが使われていない。
（2）family woman［wife］は全く使われていない。アメリカでは女性が家庭的なのは当然視されているため。

18 「愛妻家」
（ビルは愛妻家です）
Bill's ☆ Ⓐ a really loving husband.
　　　◎ Ⓑ a really caring husband.
　　　◎ Ⓒ a devoted husband.
　　　◎ Ⓓ a great［terrific］husband.

○ Ⓔ a doting husband.

19 「浮気する」
(a) 非難の気持が強い場合
（リンダは浮気しているんです）
◎ Ⓐ Linda's fucking [Linda fucks] around on her husband.
◎ Ⓑ Linda's fucking [Linda fucks] around behind her husband's back.
◎ Ⓒ Linda's screwing [Linda screws] around on her husband.
◎ Ⓓ Linda's screwing [Linda screws] around behind her husband's back.
◎ Ⓔ Linda's cheating [Linda cheats] around behind her husband's back.
◎ Ⓕ Linda's cheating [Linda cheats] on her husband.
◎ Ⓖ Linda's cheating [Linda cheats] around on her husband.
◎ Ⓗ Linda's messing [Linda messes] around on her husband.
◎ Ⓘ Linda's messing [Linda messes] around behind her husband's back.
◎ Ⓙ Linda's sleeping [Linda sleeps] around on her husband.
◎ Ⓚ Linda's sleeping [Linda sleeps] around behind her husband's back.
△ Ⓛ Linda's sneaking [Linda sneaks] around behind her husband's back.
△ Ⓜ Linda's two-timing [Linda two-times] her husband.
△ Ⓝ Linda's two-timing [Linda two-times] on her husband.
△ Ⓞ Linda's two-timing [Linda two-times] behind her husband's back.
× Ⓟ Linda's having a love affair.

[注意] (1) 批判している気持はⒶⒷが1番、ⒸⒹが2番、ⒺⒻⒼⓂⓃⓄが3番、Ⓗ～Ⓛはほぼ同じで4番。

(2) ⒶⒷは女性が男性に述べるときは、使用頻度は◎から○に下がるが、女性同士が強く批判している気持で述べるときは非常によく使われる。

(3) Ⓟが多くの辞典に出ているがこの意味では全く使われていない。「愛している」の意味ではときどき使われている。We had a love affair when we were in high school. We were in love when we were in high school. (私たちは高校生のとき愛し合っていた)

(b) 非難の気持が軽い場合
　　（ナンシーは浮気しているのよ）
　　Nancy fools ［Nancy's fooling］ ◎ Ⓐ around.
　　　　　　　　　　　　　　　　　　◎ Ⓑ around on her husband.
　　　　　　　　　　　　　　　　　　◎ Ⓒ around behind her husband's back.

(c) 客観的に述べる場合
　　（キャロルは浮気しているのよ）
　　◎ Ⓐ Carol's having an affair.
　　◎ Ⓑ Carol's having an affair on her husband.
　　○ Ⓒ Carol has an affair on her husband.
　　○ Ⓓ Carol has a man in side.

(d) 少しうらやましい気持で述べる場合
　　（バーバラは浮気しているのよ）
　　Barbara gets ［Barbara's getting］ ◎ Ⓐ around.
　　　　　　　　　　　　　　　　　　 ◎ Ⓑ around on her husband.
　　　　　　　　　　　　　　　　　　 ◎ Ⓒ around behind her husband's back.
　　　　　　　　　　　　　　　　　　 ◎ Ⓓ a little on the side.

(e) 浮気している相手の数が多いことを述べる場合
　　（リサは大勢の男性と浮気しているんです）
　　☆ Ⓐ Lisa's fooling ［Lisa fools］ around with a lot of guys.
　　◎ Ⓑ Lisa's sleeping ［Lisa sleeps］ around with a lot of guys.
　　◎ Ⓒ Lisa's messing ［Lisa messes］ around with a lot of guys.
　　◎ Ⓓ Lisa's cheating ［Lisa cheats］ around with a lot of guys.
　　◎ Ⓔ Lisa's fucking ［Lisa fucks］ around with a lot of guys.
　　◎ Ⓕ Lisa's having affairs with a lot of guys.
　　◎ Ⓖ Lisa's getting ［playing］ around with a lot of guys.
　　◎ Ⓗ Lisa's fooling ［Lisa fools］ around a lot.
　　◎ Ⓘ Lisa's sleeping ［Lisa sleeps］ around a lot.
　　◎ Ⓙ Lisa's messing ［Lisa messes］ around a lot.
　　◎ Ⓚ Lisa's cheating ［Lisa cheats］ around a lot.
　　◎ Ⓛ Lisa's fucking ［Lisa fucks］ around a lot.
　　◎ Ⓜ Lisa's having a lot of affairs.

第9章　男女間に関する表現

◎ Ⓝ Lisa's getting [Lisa gets] around a lot.
◎ Ⓞ Lisa's playing [Lisa plays] around a lot.
○ Ⓟ Lisa's screwing [Lisa screws] around with a lot of guys.
［注意］Ⓗ～Ⓞは浮気をしている人数が多いということだけでなく，同じ人だが「頻度が高い」という意味でもよく使われている。

(f) 「妻には男がいるんです」と述べる場合
（ジムの奥さんには男がいるんです）
Jim's wife ◎ Ⓐ is seeing another man.
　　　　　　○ Ⓑ has another man (on the side).
　　　　　　○ Ⓒ is seeing another man on the side.
　　　　　　○ Ⓓ has a man on the side.

20 「気が多い」
（彼女は気が多いんです）
◎ Ⓐ She's interested in a lot of guys.
× Ⓑ She's a woman of many romantic interests.
［注意］辞典にⒷが出ているが使われていない。

21 「あばずれ女」
（夫：あばずれ女）
Husband: You're ☆ Ⓐ a whore.
　　　　　　　　　◎ Ⓑ a common prostitute.
　　　　　　　　　◎ Ⓒ a slut.
　　　　　　　　　○ Ⓓ a bitch.
　　　　　　　　　○ Ⓔ loose.
［注意］責めているのはⒶⒷⒹが1番強い。2番目はⒸ，Ⓔはぐーんと弱くなる。

22 「(比喩的な意味で) つまずく」
（スティーヴは仕事ではずっと成功しているのですが，結婚でつまずいてしまったんです）
Steve's been really successful in business but he
◎ Ⓐ messed up (in) his marriage.
◎ Ⓑ messed his marriage up.
◎ Ⓒ wrecked his marriage.
◎ Ⓓ screwed up his marriage.

◎ Ⓔ screwed his marriage up.
◎ Ⓕ made a mess of his marriage.
○ Ⓖ made a wrong [bad] choice in his marriage.
○ Ⓗ made a mistake in his marriage.
△ Ⓘ made a false step in his marriage.
× Ⓙ took a wrong step [met with a setback] in his marriage.

[注意] (1) 辞典にⒿが出ているが使われていない。
(2) ⒹⒺが1番強い響きがある。2番目はⒶⒷⒻ，3番目はⒸⒼⒽⒾ
(3) Ⓖは女性のほうに非があったニュアンスがある。

23 「異性愛者」
(リンダは異性愛者です)
Linda's ☆ Ⓐ straight.
　　　　◎ Ⓑ heterosexual.

24 「両性愛者」
(リサは両性愛者です)
☆ Ⓐ Lisa's bisexual.
◎ Ⓑ Lisa goes either way.
○ Ⓒ Lisa goes both ways.

25 「同性愛」
(a) **客観的に述べるとき**
　●女性
(娘は同性愛者なんです)
My daughter's ◎ Ⓐ a homosexual.
　　　　　　　◎ Ⓑ a lesbian.
　　　　　　　◎ Ⓒ homosexual.
　　　　　　　◎ Ⓓ gay.

　●男性
(息子は同性愛者なんです)
My son's ◎ Ⓐ gay.
　　　　○ Ⓑ a homosexual.
　　　　○ Ⓒ homosexual.

(b) **否定的に述べるとき**
　●女性

(ジェーンはレズなんです)
Jane's ◎ Ⓐ a dyke.
　　　△ Ⓑ very butch.
　　　△ Ⓒ a lesbo.
●男性
(アンドルーはオカマなんです)
Andrew's ◎ Ⓐ a fag [a faggot, a queer, a homo].
　　　◎ Ⓑ queer.
　　　○ Ⓒ a flamer.
　　　○ Ⓓ a Queer.
　　　○ Ⓔ a gay-bob.
[注意] Ⓒは女装をしているオカマに使われている。Ⓓは若い男性を好む中年の男性を言うときに使われている。

(c) 「同性愛結婚」と述べるとき
(同性愛結婚は近い将来ほとんどの国で認められるでしょう)
◎ Ⓐ Same sex [Gay] marriage'll be allowed in almost all countries
× Ⓑ Same gender marriage'll be allowed ...
× Ⓒ Homosexual marriage'll be allowed ...
　　　in the near future.

第10章
暮らし・住居に関する表現

1 「暮らす」
(a) 贅沢に暮らす
   (ボブはビバリーヒルズで贅沢に暮らしています)
   Bob's ◎ Ⓐ living like a king in Beverly Hills.
   　　　 ◎ Ⓑ living extravagantly ...
   　　　 ◎ Ⓒ living luxuriously [high] ...
   　　　 ◎ Ⓓ living [leading] a luxurious life ...
   　　　 ◎ Ⓔ rolling in money [luxury] ...
   [注意] (1) He's rolling in wealth. He's living in clover. He's living like a lord [fighting cock]. He's living lapped in the luxury. He's living in the lap of luxury. He's buttering his bread on both sides. が辞典に出ているが実際にはまれにしか使われていない。
   (2) 贅沢の程度が1番高いのはⒶⒷ。

(b) 裕福に暮らす
   (彼は裕福に暮らしています)
   ☆ Ⓐ He's living well.
   ◎ Ⓑ He lives well.
   ○ Ⓒ He's living the easy life.
   ○ Ⓓ He lives the easy life.
   △ Ⓔ He's living an easy life.

(c) 快適に暮らす
   (彼は快適に暮らしています)

[120]

第10章　暮らし・住居に関する表現

　　☆ⓐ He's living comfortably.
　　◎ⓑ He lives comfortably.
　　◎ⓒ He's living a comfortable life.
　　[注意] 辞典に He's comfortably off. が出ているが使われていない。

(d)　質素に暮らす
　　（彼は質素に暮らしています）
　　He's ☆ⓐ living modestly.
　　　　　◎ⓑ living a modest life.
　　　　　○ⓒ living a simple life.
　　　　　○ⓓ living simply.

(e)　倹約して暮らす
　　（ボブは倹約して暮らしています）
　　☆ⓐ Bob's living frugally.
　　◎ⓑ Bob lives frugally.
　　◎ⓒ Bob's living a frugal life.
　　○ⓓ Bob lives a frugal life.
　　[注意] 辞典に live an economic life, live economically が出ているが使われていない。

(f)　生活力以上の暮らしをする
　　（ボブは生活力以上の暮らしをしています）
　　☆ⓐ Bob spends more than he has.
　　◎ⓑ Bob's living beyond his means.
　　△ⓒ Bob's living beyond his income.
　　△ⓓ Bob's living above his means.

2 「その日暮らしをしている」
　　（彼はキャデラックを乗っているけれど，その日暮らしなんです）
　　Even though he drives a Cadillac, he's living
　　　◎ⓐ paycheck to paycheck.
　　　○ⓑ day to day [hand to mouth].
　　　△ⓒ from paycheck to paycheck [from day to day, from hand to mouth].

3 「甲斐性がある」

[121]

(彼は甲斐性があるんです)
☆ Ⓐ He's a good provider.
☆ Ⓑ He makes a lot of money and spends it all on his family.
☆ Ⓒ He supports his family well.
◎ Ⓓ He makes a lot of money and uses it for his family.
○ Ⓔ He earns a lot of money and spends it all on his family.
[注意] Ⓐは「お金をたくさん稼ぐ」だけでなく家族のために使うというニュアンスがある。

4 「苦しい」
(私たちは生活が苦しいんです)
We're ◎ Ⓐ hurting [hard up] for money.
　　　 ◎ Ⓑ in trouble financially.
　　　 ◎ Ⓒ financially in trouble.
　　　 ◎ Ⓓ in financial trouble.
　　　 ◎ Ⓔ having a hard time financially [money-wise].
　　　 ◎ Ⓕ pressed for money.
　　　 ○ Ⓖ hurting [hard up] for cash.
　　　 ○ Ⓗ financially pressed.
　　　 ○ Ⓘ on the edge financially.

5 「生活費」
(私は生活費を切り詰めなければならないんです)
I have to cut down on my ☆ Ⓐ living expenses.
　　　　　　　　　　　　　 ◎ Ⓑ living costs.
　　　　　　　　　　　　　 ○ Ⓒ costs of living.

6 「生活水準」
(a) 維持を述べる場合
(私はこの生活水準を維持したいんです)
I want to keep this ☆ Ⓐ standard of living.
　　　　　　　　　　 ◎ Ⓑ level of living.
　　　　　　　　　　 ○ Ⓒ living standard.
　　　　　　　　　　 △ Ⓓ level of life.

(b) 高いことを述べる場合
(彼らの生活水準は私たちのより高いんです)

☆ Ⓐ They live much better than us.
☆ Ⓑ They have a higher standard of living than ours.
◎ Ⓒ Their living standard's higher than ours.
◎ Ⓓ Their standard of living's higher than ours.
◎ Ⓔ They have a higher living standard than ours.

7 「あくせくする」
(a) 仕事に対する姿勢を述べるとき
(彼は毎日あくせく働いています)
　　☆ Ⓐ He works like a slave every day.
　　◎ Ⓑ He's working like a slave every day.
　　○ Ⓒ He works like a dog every day.

(b) 問題に対する姿勢を述べるとき
(彼女は小さなことにいつもあくせくしています)
　　☆ Ⓐ She always worries about small things.
　　◎ Ⓑ She's always worrying [worried] about small things.
　　○ Ⓒ She's always worrying herself about small things.

(c) 生き方，暮らし方のような人生観を述べるとき
(彼は将来のことを心配していません。あくせくしていないんです)
He doesn't worry about his future. He's ◎ Ⓐ laid-back.
　　　　　　　　　　　　　　　　　　　◎ Ⓑ easy-going.
　　　　　　　　　　　　　　　　　　　○ Ⓒ relaxed.

8 「一文無し」
(ロンは一文無しです)
　　☆ Ⓐ Ron's flat broke.
　　◎ Ⓑ Ron hasn't got a dine [red cent].
　　○ Ⓒ Ron doesn't have a dollar to my name.
　　△ Ⓓ Ron's penniless.
　　△ Ⓔ Ron doesn't even have two nickels to rub togerher.
[注意] stone-broke, stony-broke, dead beat が辞典に出ているが使われていない。

9 「財産」
(a) 一般的に言う場合

(あの人は財産をたくさん持っています)
That guy has ◎ Ⓐ a large fortune.
　　　　　　 ◎ Ⓑ a lot of assets.
　　　　　　 ◎ Ⓒ a lot of wealth.

(b) 「財産家」と言う場合
(あの方は非常に財産家です)
☆ Ⓐ That gentleman has a lot of money.
◎ Ⓑ That gentleman's a very wealthy man.
◎ Ⓒ That gentleman's a man of great wealth.
◎ Ⓓ That gentleman's very rich.
◎ Ⓔ That gentleman has a lot of assets.
○ Ⓕ That gentleman has a large fortune.
○ Ⓖ That gentleman's a man with a large fortune.
○ Ⓗ That gentleman's a man with a lot of wealth.
△ Ⓘ That gentleman's a very rich man.
△ Ⓙ That gentleman's a man of great means [substance].
［注意］a man of means [fortune] が辞典に出ているが使われていない。

10 「階級」
(a) 上流階級
(ケリーは上流階級の出身です)
Kerry comes from ◎ Ⓐ a family with (a lot of) money.
　　　　　　　　　◎ Ⓑ a rich [welthy] family
　　　　　　　　　◎ Ⓒ the upper class.
　　　　　　　　　◎ Ⓓ an upper class family.
　　　　　　　　　◎ Ⓔ a family with old money.
　　　　　　　　　△ Ⓕ a lot of money.
［注意］(1) Ⓔは数代続いている名門という響きがある。Ⓐ～Ⓓはその点は不明。
(2) アメリカ・イギリスは日本と違って「階級社会」である。アメリカはビジネス上での成功による階級移動が可能な階級社会であるのに対して，イギリスは移動が不可能な生まれながらの階級社会。

(b) 中流の上の階級
(ビルは中流の上の階級の出身なんです)
Bill comes from ☆ Ⓐ the upper-middle class.
　　　　　　　　◎ Ⓑ the upper-middle income class [crowd].

第10章　暮らし・住居に関する表現

　　　　　◎ ⓒ upper-middle class people.
　　　　　○ ⓓ the upper-middle income bracket.
　　　　　△ ⓔ the upper-middle income segment [group].

(c) 中流階級
　（デイヴィッドは中流階級の出身です）
　David comes from ◎ ⓐ a middle income family.
　　　　　　　　　　◎ ⓑ a middle-class family.
　　　　　　　　　　◎ ⓒ a middle class.
　　　　　　　　　　○ ⓓ an average income family.
　　　　　　　　　　△ ⓔ the middle class.

(d) 中流の下の階級
　（ジョンは中流の下の階級の出身なんです）
　John comes from ◎ ⓐ the lower-middle class.
　　　　　　　　　○ ⓑ the lower-middle income bracket [group].
　　　　　　　　　○ ⓒ lower-income people.
　　　　　　　　　△ ⓓ the lower-middle income segment [class].

(e) 下層階級
　（マイクは下層階級の出身なんです）
　Mike comes from ◎ ⓐ a poor family.
　　　　　　　　　◎ ⓑ poor background.
　　　　　　　　　◎ ⓒ low income family.
　　　　　　　　　○ ⓓ low income class.
　　　　　　　　　△ ⓔ low income segment of society.
　　　　　　　　　△ ⓕ low income bracket.

(f) 貧民階級から上流階級にのし上がったとき出世話として述べる
　（彼は今では億万長者ですが下層階級の出身なんです）
　Now he's a billionaire but he came from
　　　◎ ⓐ the bad side of town.
　　　◎ ⓑ the wrong side of the tracks.
　　　◎ ⓒ a bad part of town.
　　　◎ ⓓ the inner city.
　　　○ ⓔ the other side of the tracks.

11 「マンション」

(a) 賃借しているとき
   (彼らはマンションに住んでいます)
   They live in ◎ Ⓐ an apartment (building).
             × Ⓑ an apartment house.
   [注意] 辞典にⒷが出ているが今は使われていない。

(b) 高層マンション
   (彼らはパークアベニューの高層マンションに住んでいます)
   They live in ☆ Ⓐ a high-rise on Park Avenue.
             ◎ Ⓑ a high-rise apartment (building) ...

(c) ワンルームマンション
   (マイクはワンルームマンションに住んでいます)
   Mike lives in ☆ Ⓐ a studio apartment.
               ◎ Ⓑ a studio.
               ○ Ⓒ an efficiency apartment.
               △ Ⓓ an efficiency.

(d) 分譲マンション
   (彼らはヒューロン湖が見える分譲マンションに住んでいます)
   They live in ☆ Ⓐ a condo with a view of Lake Huron.
               △ Ⓑ a condo complex ...
               △ Ⓒ a condo building ...
               △ Ⓓ a condominium ...

12 「アパート」

(a) 住んでいることを述べるとき
   (彼はアパートに住んでいます)
   He lives in ☆ Ⓐ an apartment.
             ◎ Ⓑ an apartment building.
             × Ⓒ an apartment house.
   [注意] Ⓒがどの辞典にも出ているが1980年頃から使われていない。

(b) ビル全体を述べるとき
   (彼は大きなアパートを買うつもりなんです)
   He's going to buy a big ◎ Ⓐ apartment building.

　　　　　◎ Ⓑ apartment complex.
　　　　　× Ⓒ apartment house.
［注意］(1) Ⓑは数棟のアパートのビル、またはテニスコート、プールのようなレクリエーションの設備がある1棟のアパートに使われている。
(2) 多くの辞典でⒷに「公団」の訳をつけているが誤り。「公団」の項を参照されたい。

13 「公団」
(a) **日本**
（彼らは公団に住んでいるんです）
They live in ☆ Ⓐ an apartment complex run by the government.
　　　　　 ◎ Ⓑ a government-run apartment complex.
　　　　　 ○ Ⓒ an apartment complex operated by the government.
　　　　　 ○ Ⓓ a government-operated apartment complex.

(b) **アメリカ**
（彼らは公団に住んでいます）
They live in ◎ Ⓐ a project.
　　　　　 ○ Ⓑ a housing project.
［注意］ある辞典に日本の公団には上のⒶⒷを紹介しているが次の理由で誤り。project に入居するには収入が非常に少なく、または全然ない、主として黒人ヒスパニック系の人々に建てられたもので、犯罪率が非常に高くアメリカ人は危険で暗いイメージを持っているからである。

14 「賃貸している」
(a) **家主が**
（私たちは事務所を1,000ドルで貸しています）
　◎ Ⓐ We're leasing [renting] (out) the office for [at] $1,000.
　◎ Ⓑ We lease [rent] (out) the office for [at] $1,000.

(b) **テナントが**
（私たちは事務所を1,000ドルで借りています）
　☆ Ⓐ We're renting the office for $1,000.
　◎ Ⓑ We're leasing the office for $1,000.
　○ Ⓒ We lease [rent] the office for [at] $1,000.
　○ Ⓓ We're renting [leasing] the office at $1,000.

△ Ⓔ We're renting out the office for $1,000.
× Ⓕ We're leasing out the office for $1,000.
× Ⓖ We lease [rent] out the office for $1,000.

15 「(契約が) 切れる」
(賃貸契約はこの10月に切れるんです)
The lease'll ◎ Ⓐ run out [expire] this October.
　　　　　　 ◎ Ⓑ be up ...
　　　　　　 ○ Ⓒ end ...
　　　　　　 △ Ⓓ finish [terminate, come to an end] ...
　　　　　　 ▽ Ⓔ be over [history] ...
[注意] Ⓔが辞典に出ているがこの文脈では使われてもまれである。

16 「遅れる」
(a) **毎月支払う家賃 (ローン・会費)**
　●単に遅れていることを述べる場合
(デイヴィッドは家賃が遅れているんです)
David's ◎ Ⓐ behind on [with, in] his rent.
　　　　 ◎ Ⓑ late with ...
　　　　 ○ Ⓒ late in (paying) ...
　　　　 △ Ⓓ overdue with [in] ...
　●遅れている日数・月数を述べる場合
1) 人を主語にして述べるとき
(デイヴィッドは家賃が3カ月遅れているんです)
David's three months ◎ Ⓐ behind on [with, in] his rent.
　　　　　　　　　　 ◎ Ⓑ late with ...
　　　　　　　　　　 ○ Ⓒ late in (paying) ...
　　　　　　　　　　 △ Ⓓ overdue with [in] ...
2) 家賃 (ローン・会費) を主語にして述べるとき
(デイヴィッドの家賃は3カ月遅れています)
David's rent's three months ◎ Ⓐ late.
　　　　　　　　　　　　　 ◎ Ⓑ overdue.
　　　　　　　　　　　　　 ○ Ⓒ behind.
　　　　　　　　　　　　　 △ Ⓓ slow.

17 「非常階段」
(このビルには非常階段はあるのですか)

第10章　暮らし・住居に関する表現

Does this building have ◎ Ⓐ a fire escape?
　　　　　　　　　　　 ◎ Ⓑ an emergency exit?
　　　　　　　　　　　 ○ Ⓒ an emergency stairway?
　　　　　　　　　　　 × Ⓓ an emergency stair [staircase]?

18 「クーラー」
(a) 機械に言及する場合
（ボブの事務所にはクーラーが付いていますか）
Does Bob's office have ◎ Ⓐ air-conditioning?
　　　　　　　　　　　　◎ Ⓑ an air-conditioner?
　　　　　　　　　　　　○ Ⓒ air?

(b) 稼動に言及する場合
（クーラーを弱くしておいて下さい）
Please keep ☆ Ⓐ the air down.
　　　　　　 ◎ Ⓑ the air-conditioning down.
　　　　　　 ○ Ⓒ the air-conditioner down.

19 「差し込み」
(a) 入れるとき
（電話のコードを差し込みに入れて下さい）
Please ☆ Ⓐ plug the phone in.
　　　 ◎ Ⓑ plug in [connect] the phone.
　　　 ○ Ⓒ plug the phone cord in.
　　　 ○ Ⓓ plug [connect] the phone cord into the wall.
　　　 △ Ⓔ plug the phone cord into the outlet [the wall socket].
　　　 △ Ⓕ connect the phone into the wall.
　　　 × Ⓖ insert the phone plug in the wall outlet.

(b) 抜くとき
（電話のコードを差し込みから抜いて下さい）
Please ☆ Ⓐ unplug the phone.
　　　 ◎ Ⓑ disconnect the phone.
　　　 ○ Ⓒ unplug the phone cord.
　　　 ○ Ⓓ disconnect the phone (cord) from the wall.
　　　 △ Ⓔ disconnect [unplug] the phone cord from the socket.

20「人感センサーが付いている」
　　（このアパートには人感センサーが付いているのですか）
　　Does this apartment have ◎ Ⓐ a motion senser?
　　　　　　　　　　　　　　○ Ⓑ a motion detector?

21「24時間ドアマンがいる」
　　（私たちは24時間ドアマンがいるアパートを探しています）
　　We're looking for an apartment building ☆ Ⓐ with a 24-hour
　　　　　　　　　　　　　　　　　　　　　　◎ Ⓑ that has a ...
doorman.
　　［注意］ドアマンが同時に複数いても単数形を使う。

22「ジェットバスのある」
　　（私たちはジェットバスのあるアパートを借りたいんです）
　　We want to rent an apartment ☆ Ⓐ with a wall-pool bath.
　　　　　　　　　　　　　　　　　◎ Ⓑ with a Jacuzzi.
　　　　　　　　　　　　　　　　　◎ Ⓒ that has a wall-pool bath.
　　　　　　　　　　　　　　　　　◎ Ⓓ that has a Jacuzzi.

23「栓」
(a)　栓をする
　　（浴槽に栓をして下さい）
　　☆ Ⓐ Plug the bathtub.
　　◎ Ⓑ Put the plug in the bathtub.
　　○ Ⓒ Put the stopper in the bathtub.
　　△ Ⓓ Stopper the bathtub.

(b)　栓を外す
　　（浴槽の栓を外して下さい）
　　◎ Ⓐ Unplug the bathtub.
　　◎ Ⓑ Drain the bathtub.

24「ブラインドを下ろす」
　　（ブラインドを下ろして下さい）
　　Please ☆ Ⓐ lower the blinds.
　　　　　 ☆ Ⓑ close the blinds.
　　　　　 ◎ Ⓒ put the blinds down.

第10章　暮らし・住居に関する表現

◯ Ⓓ pull the blinds down.
[注意] (1) 辞典に bring [drop, draw, haul, take] down が出ているが使われていない。
(2) ブラインドがひとつであっても普通複数形の blinds が使われている。

25 「ブラインドを上げる」
(ブラインドを上げて下さい)
☆ Ⓐ Open the blinds, please.
◎ Ⓑ Put the blinds up, ...
◎ Ⓒ Raise the blinds, ...
◯ Ⓓ Lift the blinds, ...
◯ Ⓔ Pull the blinds up, ...
[注意] 辞典に draw [haul, hold, take] up が出ているが使われていない。

26 「分譲地」
(彼らは新しい分譲地に家を買ったんです)
They bought a house in ◎ Ⓐ a new subdivision.
　　　　　　　　　　　　◎ Ⓑ a newly developed housing area.
　　　　　　　　　　　　◎ Ⓒ a new development.
　　　　　　　　　　　　◎ Ⓓ a new housing development.
　　　　　　　　　　　　◎ Ⓔ a newly developed residential area.
[注意] ⒷⒸⒹⒺは建設完了からあまり期間が過ぎていない響きがある。Ⓐは建設終了から期間が経過しているニュアンスがある。

27 「高級な（住宅街）」
(a) 2人称・3人称が主語のとき
(私の両親はシカゴの高級住宅街に住んでいます)
My parents live in ◎ Ⓐ a wealthy [a rich, a high-class, an upscale, an exclusive] neighborhood in Chicago.
　　　　　　　　　 ◯ Ⓑ an expensive ...
　　　　　　　　　 △ Ⓒ a ritzy [a classy, a swanky, a top-notch] ...
　　　　　　　　　 ▽ Ⓓ a posh [a luxurious] ...
[注意] Ⓒの swanky はアメリカの南部で使われている。

(b) 1人称が主語のとき
((不動産屋で) 私たちはサンフランシスコの周辺の高級住宅街で家を探しています)

We're looking for a house in ◎ Ⓐ an upscale [an exclusive, a nice, a good] neighborhood around San Francisco.
　　　　　　　　　　　　　　◎ Ⓑ a nice [a good] area ...
　　　　　　　　　　　　　　△ Ⓒ a classy neighborhood ...
　　　　　　　　　　　　　　× Ⓓ a wealthy [a rich, an expensive] neighborhood ...

28 「山の手」
(彼らはマンハッタンの山の手に住んでいます)
They live ◎ Ⓐ in uptown Manhattan.
　　　　　◎ Ⓑ uptown in Manhattan.
　　　　　△ Ⓒ in the uptown area of Manhattan.
　　　　　× Ⓓ in the uptown of Manhattan.

[注意]「山の手」という表現に1番近いのは uptown だが，この語には形容詞，または副詞の働きしかない。辞典には名詞の訳語が出ているが，次の文でしか使われていない。This train'll get you to uptown.（この電車は山の手へ行きます）。但し使用頻度は高くない。downtown も同様。

29 「スラム街」
(a) **一般的なスラム街**
(シカゴにはたくさんスラム街があります)
Chicago has ◎ Ⓐ a lot of slums.
　　　　　　◎ Ⓑ a lot of slum areas [neighborhoods].
　　　　　　◎ Ⓒ a lot of run-down areas [neighborhoods].
　　　　　　▽ Ⓓ a lot of slum [poor] quarters.

(b) **特定の少数民族が住んでいるスラム街**
(シカゴにはたくさんスラム街があります)
　　◎ Chicago has a lot of ghettoes.

30 「危険な」
(a) 「危険な所」と述べる場合
(危険な所を通るから油断しないで下さい)
We're going to go through
　　　◎ Ⓐ a bad neighborhood, so be alert.
　　　◎ Ⓑ a tough [rough] neighborhood, ...

◎ ⓒ the bad side of town ［the city］, ...
　　　◎ ⓓ the wrong side of town ［the city］, ...
　　　◎ ⓔ a bad part of town ［the city］, ...
　　[注意] 厳密には危険な地域が複数あるときは定冠詞の the ではなく，不定冠詞の a が正しい。しかし，この区別は守られていない。

(b) **都市・町・地域を述べる場合**
　　（クリーブランドは危険な都市です）
　　Cleveland's ◎ Ⓐ a dangerous city.
　　　　　　　　◎ Ⓑ a tough city.
　　　　　　　　◎ ⓒ a rough city.

第11章
レストラン・ホテルでの表現

1 「入る」
(a) レストラン・店などに言及する場合
   (私はジムとビルがすぐ下のレストランに入るのを見ました)
   I saw Jim and Bill ☆ Ⓐ go into the restaurant right below us.
   　　　　　　　　　　◎ Ⓑ go in ...
   　　　　　　　　　　○ Ⓒ walk into ...
   　　　　　　　　　　○ Ⓓ walk [step] in ...
   [注意] 辞典に enter が出ているが使われていない。

(b) レストラン・店などに言及しないとき
   (入りましょう)
   Let's ◎ Ⓐ walk in.
   　　　◎ Ⓑ go in.
   　　　◎ Ⓒ step in.

2 「高級レストラン」
   (たまには高級レストランで昼食を食べましょう)
   Let's have lunch at ☆ Ⓐ a fancy restaurant for a change.
   　　　　　　　　　　◎ Ⓑ a five-star restaurant ...
   　　　　　　　　　　○ Ⓒ a high-class [a ritzy, a classy, a top-notch, a fine] restaurant ...
   　　　　　　　　　　△ Ⓓ an exclusive restaurant ...
   　　　　　　　　　　× Ⓔ a quality [high-quality] restaurant ...
   [注意] Ⓑの five-star, Ⓒの top-notch が高級さの点では1番。

3 「何名様」
(何名様ですか)
☆ Ⓐ How many people're there in your group?
◎ Ⓑ How many of you're there?
◎ Ⓒ How many people're there in your party?
[注意] Ⓒは非常にかしこまった尋ね方，従って（何名様でいらっしゃいますか）という和訳に相当する。

4 「10名です」
(私たちは10名です)
☆ Ⓐ There are ten of us.
◎ Ⓑ We're a group of ten.
◎ Ⓒ We have ten people in our group.
◎ Ⓓ There are ten in our group.
◎ Ⓔ We have ten people in our party.
◎ Ⓕ There are ten people in our party.
◎ Ⓖ We're a group of ten people.
○ Ⓗ We're a party of ten.
[注意] party には改まった響きがある。

5 「…に座れますか」
(湖が見えるテーブルに座れますか)
◎ Ⓐ Can we have a table with a view of the lake?
◎ Ⓑ Can we get a table ...
○ Ⓒ Can we sit at a table ...
○ Ⓓ Is there a table ...
○ Ⓔ Do you have a table ...

6 「6人座れるテーブル」
(6人座れるテーブルはありますか)
Do you have a table for ◎ Ⓐ six?
　　　　　　　　　　　　○ Ⓑ a group of six?
　　　　　　　　　　　　○ Ⓒ a party of six?
　　　　　　　　　　　　○ Ⓓ six people?

7 「禁煙席にしていただけますか」

(禁煙席にしていただけますか)
◎ Ⓐ Can we have [get] a non-smoking table?
◎ Ⓑ Can we have [get] a no-smoking table?
◎ Ⓒ Can you give us a non-smoking [no-smoking] table?
◎ Ⓓ We'd like to have [get] a non-smoking table.
◎ Ⓔ We'd like to have [get] a no-smoking table.
○ Ⓕ We'd like a non-smoking table.
○ Ⓖ We'd like a no-smoking table.
[注意] table の代わりに area, place としても意味は同じでよく使われている。

8 「席」
(この席は空いていますか)
☆ Ⓐ Is this seat taken?
◎ Ⓑ Is somebody sitting here?
◎ Ⓒ Can I take this seat?
◎ Ⓓ Is this seat free?
◎ Ⓔ Can I have this seat?
○ Ⓕ Is this seat occupied?
○ Ⓖ Is this seat available?
[注意] Is somebody sitting on this seat? Is this seat vacant [unoccupied]? が辞典に出ているが使われてもまれ。

9 「席がある」
(あのレストランはいくつ席がありますか)
☆ Ⓐ How many tables does that restaurant have?
◎ Ⓑ How many people can that restaurant hold [seat]?
○ Ⓒ How many people can that restaurant accommmodate?
○ Ⓓ What's the seating capacity of that restaurant?
[注意] How many seats does that restaurant have? が辞典に出ているが使われていない。

10 「席を取っておく」
(これらの席を取っておいてくれますか)
Will you ☆ Ⓐ hold these tables for us?
　　　　◎ Ⓑ keep these tables for us?
　　　　◎ Ⓒ save these tables for us?

第11章 レストラン・ホテルでの表現

11「席に座らせてくれる」
（女性の案内人が湖が見える席に私たちを座らせてくれました）
The hostess ☆ Ⓐ gave us a table with a lake-view.
　　　　　　☆ Ⓑ took us to a table with a lake-view.
　　　　　　◎ Ⓒ sat us at a table with a lake-view.
　　　　　　◎ Ⓓ seated us at a table with a lake-view.

12「席を替わる」
（席を替わりましょう）
Let's ◎ Ⓐ change seats.
　　　◎ Ⓑ switch seats.
　　　○ Ⓒ trade seats.
　　　× Ⓓ exchange seats.
［注意］(1) Ⓓが辞典に出ているが使われていない。
(2) Ⓐは交換，または2人共別の席へ移る意味にもなる。ⒷⒸは交換の意味。

13「お持ち帰り」
（これはお持ち帰りですか）
A salesperson at a MacDonald's: Is this ☆ Ⓐ to go?
　　　　　　　　　　　　　　　　　　 ◎ Ⓑ for takeout?
　　　　　　　　　　　　　　　　　　 ○ Ⓒ to take out?

14「ここでお召し上がり，それともお持ち帰り」
（これはここでお召し上がりになるのですか，それともお持ち帰りになるのですか）
☆ Ⓐ For here, to go?
☆ Ⓑ For here, or to go?
◎ Ⓒ Is this here, to go?
○ Ⓓ Is this eat in, or take out?
○ Ⓔ For here, or take out?
△ Ⓕ For eat here, or to go?

15「お決りですか」
（ウエイター：ご注文はお決りですか）
Waiter: ◎ Ⓐ Are you ready to order?
　　　　◎ Ⓑ Have you decided?

　　　　◎ ⓒ Can I take your order?
　　　　○ ⓓ Can I have [get] your order?
　　　　○ ⓔ Have you decided on your order?
　　　　○ ⓕ Have you made up your mind on your order?
　　[注意] 辞典に Can I ask your order? が出ているが使われていない。

16 「料理長のおすすめ」
　　(料理長のおすすめは何ですか)
　　What's ◎ ⓐ the chef's recommendation?
　　　　　◎ ⓑ the chef's special?
　　　　　○ ⓒ the head chef's recommendation?

17 「いただきます」
　　(私はランチ A をいただきます)
　　☆ ⓐ I'll have Lunch A.
　　◎ ⓑ I'd like Lunch A.
　　◎ ⓒ I'd like to have Lunch A.
　　◎ ⓓ I'd like to order Lunch A.
　　○ ⓔ I'll eat Lunch A.
　　○ ⓕ I'd like to eat Lunch A.
　　○ ⓖ I'll order Lunch A.

18 「高級ワイン」
　　(リンダは高級ワインしか飲みません)
　　Linda only drinks ◎ ⓐ expensive [fine] wine.
　　　　　　　　　　　○ ⓑ high-quality [top-quality] ...
　　　　　　　　　　　○ ⓒ vintage ...
　　　　　　　　　　　△ ⓓ high-priced [superior] ...
　　　　　　　　　　　× ⓔ aged ...
　　[注意] (1) ⓒはワインを飲まない人の間では全く使われていない。
　　(2) ⓔが辞典に出ているが使われていない。

19 「焼く」
(a) 焼き方を尋ねる場合
　　● ステーキ
　　(ウエイター：ステーキはどのように焼きましょうか)
　　How'd you like your ☆ ⓐ steak?

　　　　　　　　　◎　Ⓑ steak done?
　　　　　　　　　◎　Ⓒ steak cooked?
　　　　　　　　　〇　Ⓓ steak fixed?
　　　　　　　　　〇　Ⓔ steak grilled?
[注意] Ⓔは open fire（直火）のときにしか使えない。ⒶⒷⒸⒹはいずれの場合でも使える。
●卵
(卵はどのように焼きましょうか)
How'd you like your ☆ Ⓐ eggs?
　　　　　　　　　◎　Ⓑ eggs cooked?
　　　　　　　　　〇　Ⓒ eggs done?
　　　　　　　　　△　Ⓓ eggs fixed?

(b) 希望する焼き方を述べる場合
　●ステーキ
(私はⒶよく焼いてⒷ普通よりよく焼いてⒸ普通に焼いてⒹ普通より生焼きでⒺ生焼きでいただきたいんです)
I'd like to have my steak Ⓐ well-done.
　　　　　　　　　　　　 Ⓑ medium-well.
　　　　　　　　　　　　 Ⓒ medium.
　　　　　　　　　　　　 Ⓓ medium-rare.
　　　　　　　　　　　　 Ⓔ rare.

　●目玉焼き
(私は卵を2つⒶ目玉焼きでⒷ目玉焼きの片面を軽く焼いていただきたいのですが)
I'd like to have two eggs ◎ Ⓐ sunny-side up.
　　　　　　　　　　　　 ◎ Ⓑ over easy.
　●ゆで卵
(私はⒶ半熟にゆでたⒷ硬くゆでた卵を2ついただきたいのですが)
I'd like to have two ◎ Ⓐ soft-boiled eggs.
　　　　　　　　　　 ◎ Ⓑ hard-boiled eggs.
　●炒り卵
(私は炒り卵を2ついただきたいのですが)
I'd like to have ☆ Ⓐ two scrambled eggs.
　　　　　　　　　◎ Ⓑ two eggs scrambled.

20 「支払う」
(a) 主語が 1 人称の場合
(私が支払います)
- ◎ Ⓐ I'll pay the check [bill, tab].
- ◎ Ⓑ I'll take care of the check [bill, tab].
- ◎ Ⓒ I'll pick up the check [bill, tab].
- ◎ Ⓓ I've got it.
- ○ Ⓔ I'll foot the check [bill, tab].

[注意] check, bill はレストラン，バーのいずれにも使われているが，tab は主としてバーで使われている。

(b) 主語が 2 人称の場合
(支払ってくれますか)
Will you ☆ Ⓐ take care of the check [bill, tab]?
　　　　 ◎ Ⓑ pay the check [bill, tab]?
　　　　 ◎ Ⓒ pick up the check [bill, tab]?
　　　　 ▽ Ⓓ foot the check [bill, tab]?

21 「どなた様のお名前でご予約する」
(どなた様のお名前でご予約なさったのですか)
- ☆ Ⓐ Whose name did you make the [a] reservation under?
- ◎ Ⓑ Whose name did you make the reservations under?
- ◎ Ⓒ Whose name is your reservation under?
- ◎ Ⓓ What name is your reservation under?
- ◎ Ⓔ What name did you make the [a] reservation under?
- ○ Ⓕ Under whose [what] name did you make the [a] reservation?

22 「予約」
(私はミケランジェロホテルに部屋を予約してあります)
- ◎ Ⓐ I have reservations [a reservation] for a room at the Michelangelo Hotel.
- ◎ Ⓑ I have a room reserved at the Michelangelo Hotel.
- ○ Ⓒ I have a room booked at the Michelangelo Hotel.

23 「予約する」
(リージェンシーホテルに部屋を予約しよう)
- ◎ Ⓐ Let's reserve a room at The Regency Hotel.

第11章　レストラン・ホテルでの表現

　　◎ Ⓑ Let's make a reservation [make reservations] for a room at The Regency Hotel.
　　○ Ⓒ Let's book a room at The Regency Hotel.
　　○ Ⓓ Let's have a room reserved at The Regency Hotel.
　　△ Ⓔ Let's make a booking for a room at The Regency Hotel.
　　△ Ⓕ Let's secure a room in advance at The Regency Hotel.
　　× Ⓖ Let's engage [bespeak] a room in advance at The Regency Hotel.
　[注意] (1) Ⓖは和英辞典に出ているが全く使われていない。
　(2) 1部屋を予約する場合でも単数，複数ともによく使われている。

24 「ルームサービス」
(a) **一般的に尋ねる場合**
　　（ルームサービスはあるのですか）
　　☆ Ⓐ Is room service available?
　　◎ Ⓑ Do you have room service?
　　◎ Ⓒ Can we get room service?
　　○ Ⓓ Is there room service available?
　　○ Ⓔ Can we use room service?
　　△ Ⓕ Are you offering room service?

(b) **深夜などに尋ねる場合**
　　（ルームサービスはまだやっているのですか）
　　☆ Ⓐ Is room service still avaible?
　　◎ Ⓑ Do you still have room service?
　　◎ Ⓒ Can we still get room service?
　　○ Ⓓ Is there room service still available?

第12章
食事・料理に関する表現

1 「食べる」
(a) 食べ始めることを述べる場合
　　●家族・友人のような人たちと家庭・レストランなどで食事をするとき
（食べましょう）
Let's ☆ Ⓐ eat.
　　　◎ Ⓑ start.
　　　○ Ⓒ dig in.
　　　△ Ⓓ begin.
　　●少しかしこまった間柄の人たちと食事をするとき
（どうぞ食べて下さい）
☆ Ⓐ Please begin.
◎ Ⓑ Bon appetit.
○ Ⓒ Please eat.
○ Ⓓ Please start.
［注意］Ⓑは厳密にはⒶⒸⒹとは違うが誤用され，ⒶⒸⒹの意味で使われている。

(b) 進行形の場合
　　（彼女は今昼食を食べています）
She's ◎ Ⓐ eating lunch now.
　　　○ Ⓑ having lunch now.

(c) 具体的に食事することを述べる場合
　　（ウエイトレス：今日は何をお召し上がりになりますか）

Waitress: What will you be ◎ Ⓐ having today?
　　　　　　　　　　　　　○ Ⓑ eating today?
[注意] have のほうが丁重に聞こえる。

(d) **ガツガツ食べる場合**
　(ガツガツ食べるな)
　Don't ☆ Ⓐ eat like a pig.
　　　　 ◎ Ⓑ eat like an animal.
　　　　 ○ Ⓒ shovel your food in.

2 「外で食べる」

(a) **単に外で食べることを述べるとき**
　(外で食べよう)
　Let's ◎ Ⓐ eat outside.
　　　　 △ Ⓑ eat al fresco.
　[注意] Ⓑは上流階級，または教育レベルの高い人の間では非常によく使われている。

(b) **昼食とか夕食に言及するとき**
　(昼食を外で食べよう)
　Let's ◎ Ⓐ eat lunch outside.
　　　　 ◎ Ⓑ have lunch outside.

3 「外食する」

　(たまには外食しよう)
　Let's ☆ Ⓐ eat out for a change.
　　　　 ○ Ⓑ eat at a restaurant for a change.
　　　　 △ Ⓒ dine out for a change.
　[注意] Ⓒは高級レストランで食べるときに使われている。ⒶⒷはレストランの質に関係なく使われている。

4 「お腹がぺこぺこ」

　(私はお腹がぺこぺこなんです)
　◎ Ⓐ I'm really hungry [starved, starving].
　◎ Ⓑ I'm starved to death.
　◎ Ⓒ I could eat a horse.
　○ Ⓓ I'm terribly hungry.

○ Ⓔ I'm fully hungry.
○ Ⓕ I'm so hungry I could eat a horse.
[注意] 辞典に I'm ravenous. I'm savagely hungry. I'm starving of hunger. が出ているが使われていない。

5 「食べ過ぎ」
（私は食べ過ぎました）
☆ Ⓐ I've had too much.
☆ Ⓑ I've had more than enough.
◎ Ⓒ I've eaten too much.
◎ Ⓓ I've eaten more than enough.

6 「満腹です」
(a) もうこれ以上食べられないという状態のとき
（私は満腹です）
I ☆ Ⓐ ate until I couldn't eat anymore.
　☆ Ⓑ stuffed my face.
　☆ Ⓒ ate too much.
　◎ Ⓓ ate until I was full.
　◎ Ⓔ ate until I could eat no more.
　◎ Ⓕ had more than enough.
　◎ Ⓖ ate more than enough.
　◎ Ⓗ had too much.
　○ Ⓘ pigged out.
　○ Ⓙ ate to my heart's content.
　△ Ⓚ ate until I was ready to burst.
[注意] 辞典に make a (good) square meal が出ているが上述の意味では使われていない。「バランスのとれた食事をする」の意味でならよく使われている。

(b) 「単に満腹です」という状態のとき
（私は満腹です）
☆ Ⓐ I'm full.
◎ Ⓑ I feel full.
◎ Ⓒ I'm feeling full.
○ Ⓓ I have a full stomach.
○ Ⓔ My stomach's full.

第12章　食事・料理に関する表現

△ Ⓕ I have a full berry.

(c) 「すごく満腹です」という状態のとき
 （私はすごく満腹です）
 ☆ Ⓐ I'm stuffed.
 ◎ Ⓑ I feel ［I'm feeling］ stuffed.
 ◎ Ⓒ I'm ［I feel］ really full.
 △ Ⓓ I have a completely full stomach.

7「少食」
 （夫は少食です）
 ☆ Ⓐ My husband doesn't eat much ［a lot］.
 ◎ Ⓑ My husband's a light eater.
 ◎ Ⓒ My husband eats verry little.
 ○ Ⓓ My husband eats like a bird.
 △ Ⓔ My husband eats a little bit ［a little, little］.

8「大食い」
 （ビルは大食いです）
 ☆ Ⓐ Bill eats a lot.
 ◎ Ⓑ Bill's a big eater.
 ◎ Ⓒ Bill really eats.
 ◎ Ⓓ Bill really eats a lot.
 ◎ Ⓔ Bill eats like a horse.
 ○ Ⓕ Bill eats very much.
 ［注意］(1) 辞典に heavy eater, heavy-eating が出ているが使われていない。
 (2) Ⓔが1番強い響きがある。Ⓓが2番，ⒶⒷⒸⒻはほぼ同じで3番。

9「料理」
(a) 広く一般的に使う場合
 （私はアメリカ料理がすごく好きです）
 I really like American ◎ Ⓐ food.
 　　　　　　　　　　× Ⓑ dishes.
 　　　　　　　　　　× Ⓒ cuisine.

(b) 洗練された料理を述べる場合
 （私はフランス料理が1番好きです）

I like French ◎ Ⓐ food best.
　　　　　　　○ Ⓑ cuisine ...
　　　　　　　△ Ⓒ dishes ...
［注意］(1) 辞典に dishes が「料理」の意味で出ているがあまり使われていない。food (料理) が繰り返されるとき，それを避ける以外は使われていない。
(2) cuisine は洗練された料理という気持が話し手にあるときには使われている。フランス料理にはよく使われている。

10 「本物の」
（私は本物のイタリア料理が食べたいんです）
I want to eat ☆ Ⓐ real Italian food.
　　　　　　　◎ Ⓑ authentic ...
　　　　　　　△ Ⓒ genuine ...

11 「好みがうるさい」
（スィンディは食べ物の好みがうるさい）
Cindy's ☆ Ⓐ picky about food.
　　　　☆ Ⓑ a picky eater.
　　　　◎ Ⓒ a fussy eater.
　　　　○ Ⓓ particular about food.
　　　　△ Ⓔ fussy [choosy] about food.

12 「甘党」
(a) 少し否定的に述べるとき
（ナンシーは甘いものに弱いんです）
Nancy ☆ Ⓐ has a sweet tooth.
　　　　◎ Ⓑ likes sweets.
　　　　○ Ⓒ has a weakness for sweets [sweet stuff].
　　　　○ Ⓓ likes sweet stuff.
　　　　△ Ⓔ likes sweet foods.

(b) 強く否定的に述べるとき
（ナンシーは甘いものを食べたらやめられないんです）
　　☆ Ⓐ Nancy's addicted to sweets.
　　☆ Ⓑ Nancy can't stop eating sweets.
　　◎ Ⓒ Nancy's hooked on sweets.

- Ⓓ Nancy can't get enough sweets.
- Ⓔ Nancy has a problem with sweets.
- Ⓕ Nancy's a sugar addict.
△ Ⓖ Nancy has trouble to stop eating sweets.

[注意] (1) 強さはⒶが1番, Ⓒが2番, Ⓕが3番, ⒺⒼが4番, ⒷⒹが5番。
(2) アメリカ人は「辛党」という発想がない。

13 「昼食を作る」
(昼食を作りましょうか)

Do you want me to ☆ Ⓐ make lunch?
◎ Ⓑ fix lunch?
○ Ⓒ cook lunch?

[注意] ⒶⒷは火を使っても使わなくても使われているが, Ⓒは火を必ず使う。

14 「食事中」
(上司は只今お得意様たちと昼食中です)

The boss's ☆ Ⓐ in the middle of lunch with our clients right now.
☆ Ⓑ having lunch ...
◎ Ⓒ eating lunch ...

[注意] ⒶはⒷⒸより「最中」というニュアンスが強い。

15 「脂肪の少ない」
(脂肪の少ない食事を取ったほうがいいですよ)

You'd better ☆ Ⓐ eat a low-fat diet.
◎ Ⓑ eat low-fat food.
◎ Ⓒ stay on [get on] a low-fat diet.
○ Ⓓ eat low-fat meals.
○ Ⓔ follow a low-fat diet.

[注意] diet には「a」が付くが, food には「a」が付かない。

16 「脂肪のない」
(私は脂肪のない食事を取っています)

☆ Ⓐ I'm on a fat-free diet.
◎ Ⓑ I'm on a no-fat diet.
○ Ⓒ I'm staying [following] a fat-free diet.
○ Ⓓ I only eat food without fat.
○ Ⓔ I'm on a non-fat diet.

［注意］辞典に I'm on a fatless diet が出ているが使われていない。

17 「ノンオイルの」
(私はノンオイルのドレッシングを使っています)
I use ☆ Ⓐ non-fat dressing.
　　　◎ Ⓑ no-fat ...
　　　× Ⓒ no-oil ...

18 「あぶらっこい」
(a)　料理の内容
(あぶらっこすぎるから私はステーキは避けています)
I stay away from steak because ☆ Ⓐ it has too much fat.
　　　　　　　　　　　　　　　　◎ Ⓑ it's too fatty.
　　　　　　　　　　　　　　　　× Ⓒ it has too much oil.
　　　　　　　　　　　　　　　　× Ⓓ it has too much grease.
　　　　　　　　　　　　　　　　× Ⓔ it's too greasy.

(b)　料理の仕方
(あぶらっこすぎるから私はフライドチキンは避けています)
I stay away from fried chicken because
　　　◎ Ⓐ it's too greasy.
　　　◎ Ⓑ it has too much grease.
　　　◎ Ⓒ it has too much grease on it.
　　　× Ⓓ it has too much oil.
　　　× Ⓔ it has too much fat.
　　　× Ⓕ it's too fatty.
［注意］チキンの中には fat がないと考えられている。

19 「あぶらっこい」
(イタリアンドレッシングはあぶらっこすぎます)
　　　☆ Ⓐ Italian dressing's too oily.
　　　◎ Ⓑ Italian dressing has too much oil in it.
　　　◎ Ⓒ Italian dressing has too much oil.
　　　◯ Ⓓ Italian dressing has too much fat.
　　　◯ Ⓔ Italian dressing has too much fat in it.

20 「こってりした」

(a) **量は少ないがカロリーのある料理**
　　（フランス料理は非常にこってりしています）
　　◎ French food's really rich.
　　[**注意**] 辞典に Chinese food's rich. と出ているが次の理由で誤り。
　　(1) rich とは甘いケーキ，ペイストリー，またはソースの濃い料理にしか使えない。
　　(2) 中国料理はアメリカ人にとってこってりした料理ではない。

(b) **量もカロリーもある料理**
　　（イタリア料理はこってりしています）
　　Italian food's ☆ Ⓐ heavy.
　　　　　　　　 ◎ Ⓑ very filling.

21 「辛い」

(a) **料理**
　　（メキシコ料理は辛いです）
　　Mexican food's ◎ Ⓐ hot.
　　　　　　　　　 ◎ Ⓑ spicy.

(b) **チーズ**
　　（グレッグは辛いチーズが好きです）
　　Greg likes ◎ Ⓐ sharp cheese.
　　　　　　　 ○ Ⓑ tangy cheese.
　　　　　　　 △ Ⓒ spicy cheese.

(c) **ドレッシング**
　　（ロンは辛いドレッシングが好きです）
　　Ron likes ☆ Ⓐ tangy dressing.
　　　　　　　◎ Ⓑ spicy dressing.
　　　　　　　× Ⓒ sharp dressing.
　　[**注意**] Ⓒが辞典に出ているが使われていない。

(d) **ワイン**
　　（ブライアンは辛いワインが好きです）
　　Brian likes ◎ Ⓐ dry wine.
　　　　　　　　× Ⓑ spicy wine.
　　　　　　　　× Ⓒ hot wine.

22「塩辛い」
　　（このスープは塩辛すぎる）
　　☆ Ⓐ This soup's too salty.
　　◎ Ⓑ There's too much salt in this soup.
　　◎ Ⓒ This soup has too much salt (in it).

23「すっぱい」
　　（私はすっぱい食べ物は嫌いです）
　　I don't like ◎ Ⓐ sour food.
　　　　　　　　○ Ⓑ acidic food.

24「炭水化物の少ない食事」
　　（医師：あなたは炭水化物の少ない食事を食べたほうがいいですよ）
　　Doctor: You'd better ☆ Ⓐ not eat so many carbohydrates.
　　　　　　　　　　　　☆ Ⓑ cut down on carbohydrates.
　　　　　　　　　　　　◎ Ⓒ eat a low-carbohydrate diet.
　　　　　　　　　　　　◎ Ⓓ eat low-carbohydrate foods.
　　　　　　　　　　　　△ Ⓔ a diet with little carbohydrate.
　　　　　　　　　　　　△ Ⓕ a diet that has little carbohydrate (in it).

25「糖分のない」
　　（私は糖分のない食事を取っています）
　　☆ Ⓐ I'm on a sugar-free diet.
　　☆ Ⓑ I'm on a no-sugar diet.
　　◎ Ⓒ I can only eat food without sugar.
　　○ Ⓓ I'm on a sugerless diet.
　　○ Ⓔ I'm on a non-sugar diet.

26 塩分の多い
　　（塩分の多い食物は避けておきなさい）
　　Stay away from ◎ Ⓐ salty food.
　　　　　　　　　○ Ⓑ food with a lot of salt.

27「塩分が非常に多い」
　　（医師：あなたは塩分が非常に多い料理を避けたほうがいいですよ）
　　Doctor: You'd better stay away from ☆ Ⓐ really salty food.

　　　　　　　　　　　◎ Ⓑ food with a lot of salt
　　　　　　　　　　　　　(in it).
　　　　　　　　　　　◎ Ⓒ food that has a lot of
　　　　　　　　　　　　　salt (in it).

28「（塩・コショウ・マスタードなどを）とる」
　（お塩をとってくれますか）
　Will you ☆ Ⓐ pass me the salt?
　　　　　　◎ Ⓑ get me the salt?

29「コーヒーを入れる」
　（コーヒーを入れましょうか）
　Do you want me to ◎ Ⓐ make some coffee?
　　　　　　　　　　○ Ⓑ fix some coffee?
　　　　　　　　　　△ Ⓒ brew some coffee?

30「（悪い状態に）なる」
　（ミルクを冷蔵庫に入れなさい，さもないと悪くなるでしょう）
　Put the milk in the fridge, or it'll ◎ Ⓐ turn sour.
　　　　　　　　　　　　　　　　　　 ◎ Ⓑ get sour.
　　　　　　　　　　　　　　　　　　 △ Ⓒ become [go, be] sour.
　［注意］turn 及び go が「なる」の意味で使われるのはよくない状態に「なる」場合である。

31「（アルコール）飲む」
(a)　普通に述べる場合
　（ビルはアルコールは飲みません）
　Bill ☆ Ⓐ doesn't drink.
　　　 ◎ Ⓑ doesn't drink liquor [alcohol].
　　　 ◎ Ⓒ doesn't touch liquor [alcohol].
　　　 ○ Ⓓ doesn't touch the stuff.

(b)　強調して述べる場合
　（ビルは全くアルコールは飲みません）
　Bill ☆ Ⓐ never drinks.
　　　 ☆ Ⓑ doesn't drink at all.
　　　 ◎ Ⓒ doesn't drink a drop.

[**注意**] 辞典に be a strict teetotaler, be strict teetotal, abstain from alcohol が出ているが使われていない。

32 「久し振りに飲む」
(久し振りにビールを飲んでいるんですよ)
- ◎ Ⓐ This is the first beer I've had in ages [in a long time].
- ◎ Ⓑ This is my first beer in ages [in a long time].
- △ Ⓒ This is the first beer I've had in a long while.
- △ Ⓓ This is my first beer in a long while.
- × Ⓔ I'm drinking beer after a long abstinence.

[**注意**] Ⓔが辞典に出ているが使われていない。

33 「酒を飲むとすぐ酔っ払う」
(彼は酒を飲むとすぐ酔っ払うんです)
- ◎ Ⓐ He can't hold his liquor [alcohol].
- ◯ Ⓑ He gets drunk easily.
- ◯ Ⓒ Liquor [Alcohol] goes to his head fast.
- ◯ Ⓓ Liquor [Alcohol] goes to his head quick.

34 「酒を飲んでもすぐ酔わない」
(彼は酒を飲んでもすぐ酔わないんです)
- ◎ Ⓐ He can really hold his liquor.
- ◯ Ⓑ He doesn't get drunk easily.
- ◯ Ⓒ Liquor [Alcohol] doesn't go to his head fast.
- ◯ Ⓓ Liquor [Alcohol] doesn't go to his head quick.

35 「飲ん兵衛」
(ブライアンは飲ん兵衛だ)

Brian's
- ◎ Ⓐ a heavy drinker.
- ◯ Ⓑ a boozer.
- △ Ⓒ a drunkard.
- ▽ Ⓓ a tipper.
- × Ⓔ a sot [a drunk, sot, a souse].

[**注意**] Ⓔが辞典に出ているが使われていない。

第13章

買物に関する表現

1 「安い」

(a) 品物が主語の場合
(あのビロードの襟が付いたグレーのオーバーはどう。あれは安いです)
How do you like that gray coat with the velvet collar?
　　☆ Ⓐ It's cheap.
　　☆ Ⓑ It's a good buy.
　　◎ Ⓒ It's not expensive.
　　○ Ⓓ It's inexpensive.
［注意］Ⓐの cheap は「安い」だけでなく「安っぽい」という意味もある。従って店員は使わない。しかし，お客は非常によく使う。

(b) 料金・税金のような無形物が主語の場合
(この弁護士の着手金は安いね)
This lawyer's retainer's ◎ Ⓐ low.
　　　　　　　　　　　　△ Ⓑ inexpensive [cheap].

(c) 比較級・最上級の場合
(これはあれより安いです)
This is ◎ Ⓐ less expensive than that.
　　　　◎ Ⓑ cheaper than that.
　　　　× Ⓒ more inexpensive than that.
［注意］(1) Ⓑは店員などには使われていない。
(2) inexpensive を比較級として more inexpensive とはしない。Ⓐのように less expensive とする。

[153]

(d) 「いい買物」というニュアンスの「安い」
　　●普通に言うとき
　　（営業マン：この車はいい買物ですよ）
　　This car's ◎ Ⓐ a good buy.
　　　　　　　 ◎ Ⓑ a good deal.
　　　　　　　 ○ Ⓒ a (good) bargain.
　　[注意]「安い」という度合の点ではⒸが1番，2番目はⒷ，3番目はⒶ。

　　●少し強調して言うとき
　　（営業マン：この車はすごくいい買物ですよ）
　　This car's ◎ Ⓐ a great deal [buy, bargain].
　　　　　　　 ◎ Ⓑ a steal.
　　　　　　　 ○ Ⓒ a real bargain.

　　●非常に強調して言うとき
　　（営業マン：この車はものすごくいい買物ですよ）
　　This car's ◎ Ⓐ an incredible [a real] deal.
　　　　　　　 ◎ Ⓑ a fantastic deal.
　　　　　　　 ◎ Ⓒ a wonderful [terrific] deal.
　　　　　　　 ◎ Ⓓ a great deal.
　　　　　　　 ◎ Ⓔ an incredibe bargain.
　　　　　　　 ◎ Ⓕ a real bargain.
　　　　　　　 ◎ Ⓖ a fantastic [great] bargain.
　　　　　　　 ◎ Ⓗ a wonderful [terrific] bargain.
　　　　　　　 ◎ Ⓘ an incredibe buy.
　　　　　　　 ◎ Ⓙ a fantastic buy.
　　　　　　　 ◎ Ⓚ a wonderful [terrific] buy.
　　　　　　　 △ Ⓛ a dirt cheap.
　　[注意] (1) Ⓛは話し手が客ならば非常によく使われている。
　　(2) 強さの点ではⒶⒺⒾⓁが1番，ⒷⒻⒿが2番，ⒸⒽⓀが3番，ⒹⒼが4番。

2 「安くする」
　　（私にこの車を少し安くしてくれますか）
　　Can you ☆ Ⓐ come down a little on the price of this car?
　　　　　　 ◎ Ⓑ give me a little better deal on this car?
　　　　　　 ◎ Ⓒ lower the price a little on this car?
　　　　　　 ◎ Ⓓ give me a little lower price on this car?

　　　　　◎ Ⓔ go down a little on the price of this car?
　　　　　◯ Ⓕ come down a little on this car?
　　　　　◯ Ⓖ give me a little better price on this car?
　[注意] Ⓑの better deal は値段以外の保険なども意味されることもあるが、値段だけの意味でもよく使われている。

3 「ぎりぎりの値段です」
　（営業マン：それがぎりぎりの値段ですね）
　That's ☆ Ⓐ the best price we can ［could］ give you.
　　　　　☆ Ⓑ the lowest price ...
　　　　　◎ Ⓒ our best ［lowest］ price ...
　　　　　◎ Ⓓ our bottom price ...
　　　　　◯ Ⓔ the bottom price ...

4 「サービス」
(a) 一般の店で
　（これらをサービスしておきます）
　☆ Ⓐ You can have these for free.
　◎ Ⓑ You can have these free of charge.
　◯ Ⓒ You can have these for nothing.
　◯ Ⓓ You can have these without charge.
　× Ⓔ We'll give you these for nothing.

(b) 高級店で
　（これらをサービスさせていただきます）
　You may have these ☆ Ⓐ for free.
　　　　　　　　　　　◎ Ⓑ free of charge.
　　　　　　　　　　　◯ Ⓒ for nothing.
　　　　　　　　　　　◯ Ⓓ without charge.

5 「ちょうど」
　（レジ：ちょうど200ドルです）
　Cashier: ☆ Ⓐ Exactly $200.
　　　　　 ◎ Ⓑ $200 even.
　　　　　 ◎ Ⓒ Even $200.
　　　　　 × Ⓓ Around $200.
　　　　　 × Ⓔ $200 on the mark.

　　　　× Ⓕ Just $200.
　　[注意] 辞典にⒹⒺⒻが出ているが使われていない。

6「営業時間」
　　（営業時間は何時から何時までですか）
　　☆ Ⓐ What're your store hours?
　　☆ Ⓑ When're you open?
　　◎ Ⓒ What're your hours?
　　◎ Ⓓ What hours're you open?
　　○ Ⓔ What're your business hours?
　　○ Ⓕ When's your business open?

7「看板です（閉店です）」
　　（皆さん，看板です）
　　Everybody, ☆ Ⓐ it's closing time.
　　　　　　　　◎ Ⓑ we're closing.
　　　　　　　　◎ Ⓒ closing time.
　　　　　　　　○ Ⓓ time to close.
　　[注意] 辞典に Everybody, time. が出ているがまれにしか使われていない。

8「看板を出す」
　　（看板を出したほうがいいですよ）
　　You better ☆ Ⓐ put up your sign.
　　　　　　　　☆ Ⓑ set up your sign.
　　　　　　　　◎ Ⓒ hang your sign up.
　　　　　　　　○ Ⓓ hang out your sign.
　　[注意] (1) 辞典に signboard が出ているが使われていない。
　　(2) 自分の店，会社以外，つまり第三者の屋上，土地などに出させてもらっている看板は billboard.

9「看板」
　　（あなたの店の看板は出ているのですか）
　　☆ Ⓐ Does your store have a sign?
　　☆ Ⓑ Is there a sign on your store?
　　◎ Ⓒ Does your store have a sign up?
　　◎ Ⓓ Is your store a sign up?
　　○ Ⓔ Does your store have a sign out?

第14章

道順に関する表現

1「ここはどこですか」
（おまわりさん，ここはどこですか）
Officer, ☆ Ⓐ what street is this?
　　　　　◎ Ⓑ what street am I on?
　　　　　○ Ⓒ where am I?
　　　　　○ Ⓓ what place is this?

2「信号」
（郵便局は信号から3番目のビルの中にあります）
The post office is in the third building from
　　☆ Ⓐ the light.
　　◎ Ⓑ the stoplight.
　　○ Ⓒ the traffic light.
　　△ Ⓓ the traffic signal.

3「歩いて下さい」
（最初の信号までこの道を歩いて下さい）
◎ Ⓐ Go down this street until you get to the first light.
◎ Ⓑ Walk down ...
○ Ⓒ Go up ...
○ Ⓓ Walk up ...
○ Ⓔ Go along ...
○ Ⓕ Walk along ...
[注意] Ⓐ，Ⓒ，Ⓔは歩いている人，車を運転している人の両方に使える。

4 「この先」
(a) 通りの数ブロック先
　　（フランス大使館はこの先です）
　　The French Embassy's ☆ Ⓐ down the street ［road］.
　　　　　　　　　　　　　◎ Ⓑ up the street ［road］.
　　　　　　　　　　　　　◎ Ⓒ further (up) ahead.
　　　　　　　　　　　　　◎ Ⓓ up ahead.

(b) 同じブロックの場合
　　●ブロックが大きいとき
　　（ギリシア領事館はこの先です）
　　The Greek Consulate's ☆ Ⓐ down the block ［street, road］.
　　　　　　　　　　　　　　◎ Ⓑ up the block ［street, road］.
　　●ブロックが小さいとき
　　（カノヴァ保険はこの先です）
　　Canover Insurance is ☆ Ⓐ down the block.
　　　　　　　　　　　　　◎ Ⓑ up the block.

(c) 「この少し先」の場合
　　（国税庁はこの少し先です）
　　The IRS building's ☆ Ⓐ just down the street.
　　　　　　　　　　　☆ Ⓑ a little way(s) down the street.
　　　　　　　　　　　◎ Ⓒ just up the street.
　　　　　　　　　　　◎ Ⓓ a little way(s) up the street.

(d) 「このずっと先」の場合
　　（出入国管理局はこのずっと先です）
　　Immigration's ◎ Ⓐ a long way(s) down the street.
　　　　　　　　　◎ Ⓑ way down the street.
　　　　　　　　　○ Ⓒ a long way(s) up the street.
　　　　　　　　　○ Ⓓ way up the street.

5 「数軒先」
　　（彼の事務所は国税庁から数軒先です）
　　His office is a few doors ☆ Ⓐ down from the IRS building.
　　　　　　　　　　　　　　　◎ Ⓑ away from ...

第14章　道順に関する表現

　　　　　　◎ Ⓒ past from ...
　　　　　　○ Ⓓ up from ...

6 「…の少し先」
　　（英国大使館は市役所の少し先です）
　　The British Embassy's ☆ Ⓐ a little past town hall.
　　　　　　　　　　　　◎ Ⓑ just a little past ...
　　　　　　　　　　　　◎ Ⓒ a little bit past ...
　　　　　　　　　　　　◎ Ⓓ just past ...
　　　　　　　　　　　　○ Ⓔ just a little after ...
　　　　　　　　　　　　○ Ⓕ a little after ...
　　[注意] town hall は「町役場」だけでなく「市役所」の意味でもよく使われている。

7 「この通りの少し先」
　　（ニューヨーク大学はこの通りの少し先です）
　　New York University's ☆ Ⓐ just down the street.
　　　　　　　　　　　　◎ Ⓑ a little bit ［a little way(s)］ down the street.
　　　　　　　　　　　　○ Ⓒ a little down the street.
　　　　　　　　　　　　○ Ⓓ just a little down ［up］ the street.
　　　　　　　　　　　　○ Ⓔ just a bit down ［up］ the street.

8 「少し手前」
　　（図書館は市役所の少し手前です）
　　The library's ☆ Ⓐ just before city hall.
　　　　　　　　◎ Ⓑ a little before ...
　　　　　　　　◎ Ⓒ a little bit before ...
　　　　　　　　○ Ⓓ just a little before ...

9 「突き当たった所に」
(a)　**通り**
　　（市役所はこの通りの突き当たった所にあります）
　　City Hall's ◎ Ⓐ all the way down the street.
　　　　　　　◎ Ⓑ at the end of ...
　　　　　　　○ Ⓒ all the way up ...

[159]

(b) ビルの中
(ブラウン法律事務所はこの廊下の突き当たった所にあります)
Brown Law Firm's ☆ Ⓐ all the way down the hall.
　　　　　　　　　◎ Ⓑ at the end of ...
　　　　　　　　　○ Ⓒ all the way up ...

10 「そばに」
(彼女は私のそばで食事をしていました)
She was eating ☆ Ⓐ next to me.
　　　　　　　　◎ Ⓑ beside me.
　　　　　　　　○ Ⓒ by me.
[注意] ⒶⒷのほうがⒸより近いニュアンスがある。

11 「すぐそばに」
(うちの事務所のすぐそばに大きな駐車場があります)
There's a big parking lot ☆ Ⓐ right by our office.
　　　　　　　　　　　　　◎ Ⓑ right near our office.
　　　　　　　　　　　　　○ Ⓒ just by our office.
　　　　　　　　　　　　　○ Ⓓ just near our office.

12 「そばを」
(私たちは毎日郵便局のそばを車で通ります)
We drive ◎ Ⓐ by the post office every day.
　　　　　◎ Ⓑ past the post office every day.

13 「真裏に」
(ラッセル証券会社の真裏にバイキングレストランがあります)
There's an all-you-can eat restaurant
　　◎ Ⓐ right [directly] behind Russel Trading Company.
　　○ Ⓑ immediately behind ...
　　○ Ⓒ right in back of ...
　　▽ Ⓓ just [directly, immediately] in back of...

14 「(…の) 真向いに」
(彼の店はマーティン旅行代理店の真向いにあります)
　　☆ Ⓐ His store's right [just] across (the street) from Martin Travel Agency.

◎ Ⓑ His store's directly [immediately] across (the street) from ...
◎ Ⓒ His store's right [just, directly, immediately] on the other side of the street from ...
◎ Ⓓ His store's right [just, directly, immediately] on the opposite side of the street from ...
◎ Ⓔ His store faces ...
○ Ⓕ His store's right [just, directly, immediately] opposite ...

15 「下の階の」
(下の階のレストランへ行こう)
☆ Ⓐ Let's go to the restaurant downstairs.
◎ Ⓑ Let's go downstairs to the restaurant.
○ Ⓒ Let's go to the restaurant below us.
△ Ⓓ Let's go to the restaurant under us.
△ Ⓔ Let's go to the restaurant on the lower level.
[注意] ⒶⒷⒸⒹⒺは1階下なのか数階下なのかは不明。

16 「すぐ下の階の」
(すぐ下の階のレストランへ行こう)
Let's go to the restaurant ☆ Ⓐ right downstairs.
　　　　　　　　　　　　　◎ Ⓑ just downstairs.
　　　　　　　　　　　　　◎ Ⓒ right [just] below us.
　　　　　　　　　　　　　◎ Ⓓ one flight [floor] down.
　　　　　　　　　　　　　○ Ⓔ right [just] under us.

17 「上の階の」
(上の階のレストランへ行こう)
☆ Ⓐ Let's go to the restaurant upstairs.
◎ Ⓑ Let's go upstairs to the restaurant.
○ Ⓒ Let's go to the restaurant above us.
○ Ⓓ Let's go to the restaurant on the upper level.
△ Ⓔ Let's go to the restaurant over us.
[注意] ⒶⒷⒸⒹⒺは1階上なのか数階上なのかは不明。

18 「すぐ上の階の」
(すぐ上の階のレストランへ行こう)
Let's go to the restaurant ☆ Ⓐ right upstairs.

◎ Ⓑ just upstairs.
◎ Ⓒ right ［just］ above us.
◎ Ⓓ one flight ［floor］ up.
○ Ⓔ right ［just］ over us.

19 「途中で」
(a) …へ行く途中で
（私は市役所へ行く途中でジムに偶然会いました）
I bumped into Jim ☆ Ⓐ on the way to city hall.
　　　　　　　　　☆ Ⓑ on my way to …
　　　　　　　　　◎ Ⓒ while I was going to …
　　　　　　　　　◎ Ⓓ when I was going to …

(b) …からの帰宅途中で
（私は職場からの帰宅途中でビルに偶然会いました）
I ran into Bill ☆ Ⓐ on my ［the］ way home from work.
　　　　　　　◎ Ⓑ on my ［the］ way back home …
　　　　　　　◎ Ⓒ on my ［the］ way back …
　　　　　　　◎ Ⓓ while ［when］ I was on my ［the］ way home …
　　　　　　　◎ Ⓔ while I was going home …
　　　　　　　△ Ⓕ on the way to my ［the］ house …

第15章
交通機関に関する表現

1「…で通勤する」
(a) 電車, バスなどで
　（私は毎日地下鉄で通勤しています）
　I ☆ Ⓐ take the subway to work every day.
　　◎ Ⓑ ride ...
　　△ Ⓒ use ...
　　△ Ⓓ catch ...

(b) 車で
　（私は毎日車で通勤しています）
　I ☆ Ⓐ drive to work every day.
　　○ Ⓑ go [commute] to work by car every day.
　　○ Ⓒ take my car to work every day.
　　△ Ⓓ travel to work by car every day.

(c) 帰宅の方法も言及する場合
　●電車, バスなどで
　（私は毎日職場へ地下鉄で通勤しています）
　I ☆ Ⓐ take the subway to and from work every day.
　　◎ Ⓑ ride ...
　　△ Ⓒ use ...
　　△ Ⓓ catch ...

　●車で

[163]

(私は毎日車で職場へ通勤しています)
I ☆ Ⓐ drive both ways to work every day.
　　◎ Ⓑ drive to and from work ...
　　○ Ⓒ drive back and forth between my house and work ...
　　○ Ⓓ travel both ways to work by car ...

2 「乗る」
(a) 命令・提案
　(あの電車に乗りなさい)
　◎ Ⓐ Take that train.
　◎ Ⓑ Catch that train.
　◎ Ⓒ Get on that train.
　○ Ⓓ Ride on that train.
　○ Ⓔ Ride that train.
　△ Ⓕ Board [Use] that train.

(b) 乗る駅名を明示する場合
　(42丁目からフラッシャイニング線に乗りなさい)
　◎ Ⓐ Take the Flushining Line from 42nd St.
　○ Ⓑ Use [Ride on, Ride] the Flushining Line ...
　○ Ⓒ Catch the Flushining Line ...
　○ Ⓓ Get on the Flushining Line ...

(c) 目的地を明示する場合
　(私たちはウォール街まで地下鉄に乗って行きました)
　We ◎ Ⓐ took the subway to Wall Street.
　　　○ Ⓑ rode the subway ...
　　　△ Ⓒ rode on [use] the subway ...

(d) 乗っている状態に言及する場合
　(リズは私と同じ電車に乗っていました)
　Liz was ◎ Ⓐ taking the same train as I was.
　　　　　◎ Ⓑ on the same train ...
　　　　　○ Ⓒ riding (on) the same train ...

(e) 行先を尋ねる場合
　(どこまで急行に乗って行ったのですか)

Where did you ☆ Ⓐ take the experess to?
　　　　　　 ☆ Ⓑ ride the experess to?
　　　　　　 ◎ Ⓒ take the experess?
　　　　　　 ○ Ⓓ ride the experess?

(f) **乗った駅名を尋ねる場合**
（あなたはどこで地下鉄に乗ったのですか）
Where did you ◎ Ⓐ catch the subway?
　　　　　　 ◎ Ⓑ get on the subway?
　　　　　　 △ Ⓒ catch [get on] the subway at?

(g) **「乗ったことがある」という経験を述べる場合**
● 地下鉄
（私はマンハッタンで地下鉄に乗ったことがありません）
I've never ◎ Ⓐ taken the subway in Manhattan.
　　　　　 ◎ Ⓑ been on the subway ...
　　　　　 ◎ Ⓒ used the subway ...
　　　　　 ○ Ⓓ ridden the subway ...
　　　　　 △ Ⓔ ridden on the subway ...

● タクシー
（あなたはロサンジェルスでタクシーに乗ったことがありますか）
Have you ever ◎ Ⓐ taken a cab in Los Angeles?
　　　　　　 ◎ Ⓑ been in a cab ...
　　　　　　 ◎ Ⓒ used a cab ...
　　　　　　 ○ Ⓓ taken a ride in a cab ...

● 飛行機
1) 一般的に言うとき
（リンダは飛行機に乗ったことがありますか）
Has Linda ever ☆ Ⓐ flown?
　　　　　　　 ◎ Ⓑ been [traveled] on a plane?
　　　　　　　 ◎ Ⓒ taken a flight?
　　　　　　　 ○ Ⓓ ridden on a plane?
　　　　　　　 △ Ⓔ ridden a plane?
　　　　　　　 × Ⓕ used a plane?
2) 航空会社を明示したいとき

(あなたはデルタに乗ったことがありますか)
Have you ever ◎ Ⓐ flown on [flown with] Delta?
　　　　　　 ◎ Ⓑ taken [gone on] a Delta flight?
　　　　　　 ◎ Ⓒ used Delta?
　　　　　　 ◎ Ⓓ been [traveled] on Delta?
　　　　　　 ○ Ⓔ ridden on Delta?
　　　　　　 △ Ⓕ ridden [traveled with] Delta?

3) 等級を明示したいとき
(私はファーストクラスの飛行機に乗ったことはありません)
I've never ☆ Ⓐ flown first class.
　　　　　 ☆ Ⓑ traveled [flown in, sat in] first class.
　　　　　 ○ Ⓒ sat in first class on a plane.
　　　　　 ○ Ⓓ traveled in a first class seat.
　　　　　 △ Ⓔ traveled in the first class section.
　　　　　 △ Ⓕ taken a first class seat on a plane.

3 「乗り換える」

(42丁目で電車を乗り換えなさい)
☆ Ⓐ Change trains at 42nd St.
◎ Ⓑ Switch trains at 42nd St.
◎ Ⓒ Transfer at 42nd St.

4 「(交通機関が) …へ行く」

(このバスは市役所へ行きますか)
Does this bus ☆ Ⓐ go to city hall?
　　　　　　　◎ Ⓑ take me to city hall?
　　　　　　　○ Ⓒ get me to city hall?
　　　　　　　○ Ⓓ bring me to city hall?

5 「(…に) 乗り換える」

(私はユニオン駅で地下鉄に乗り換えます)
I'm going to ◎ Ⓐ change [transfer, switch] to the subway at Union Station.
　　　　　　 ◎ Ⓑ change [switch] trains to the subway at Union Station.
　　　　　　 ◎ Ⓒ change [switch] trains at Union Station to the subway.

第15章　交通機関に関する表現

　　　　　　△ ⒟ change trains at Union Station for the subway.

6「(このまま)乗っていく」
　　(僕は42丁目まで(このまま)この電車に乗っていくよ)
　　I'm going to ☆ Ⓐ take this train to 42nd St.
　　　　　　　　◎ Ⓑ stay on this train to ...
　　　　　　　　◎ Ⓒ stay on this train until ...
　　　　　　　　◯ ⒟ be on this train to ...
　　　　　　　　△ Ⓔ be on this train until ...

7「何番目」
　　(コロンバスサークルは何番目の駅ですか)
　　How many stations ☆ Ⓐ to Columbus Circle?
　　　　　　　　　　　◎ Ⓑ are there between here and ...
　　　　　　　　　　　◎ Ⓒ until ...
　　　　　　　　　　　◯ ⒟ are there to ...
　　　　　　　　　　　◯ Ⓔ are there until ...
　　　　　　　　　　　◯ Ⓕ are there before ...
　　　　　　　　　　　◯ Ⓖ is it to ...
　　　　　　　　　　　△ Ⓗ come before ...

8「乗り越す」
　　(昨夜私は読書に非常に夢中になっていたので乗り越してしまったんです)
　　Last night I was so absorbed in my reading I
　　　◎ Ⓐ went past my stop.
　　　◎ Ⓑ went beyond my stop.
　　　◎ Ⓒ rode past my stop.
　　　▽ ⒟ went beyond [past] my destination.
　　　✕ Ⓔ was carried beyond my stop.
　　　✕ Ⓕ overshot my stop.
　　［注意］ⒺⒻが辞典に出ているが使われていない。

9「(…行きと)書いてある」
　　(リンカーンセンターと書いてある電車に乗って下さい)
　　Take the train ☆ Ⓐ that says Lincoln Center.
　　　　　　　　　◎ Ⓑ with the sign that says ...
　　　　　　　　　◯ Ⓒ saying ...

[167]

○ Ⓓ with the sign to ...

10「…まわり（経由）で」
(新宿まわりで池袋に行こう)
Let's go to Ikebukuro ☆ Ⓐ that goes through Shinjuku.
　　　　　　　　　　　◎ Ⓑ that stops at ...
　　　　　　　　　　　◎ Ⓒ that stops in ...
　　　　　　　　　　　○ Ⓓ by way of ...
　　　　　　　　　　　○ Ⓔ through ...
　　　　　　　　　　　△ Ⓕ via ...

11「直行する」
(市役所へ直行する電車はありません)
There's no train that'll ☆ Ⓐ take you directly to city hall.
　　　　　　　　　　　☆ Ⓑ take you straight to city hall.
　　　　　　　　　　　◎ Ⓒ get you directly to city hall.
　　　　　　　　　　　◎ Ⓓ get you straight to city hall.
　　　　　　　　　　　○ Ⓔ bring you directly to city hall.
　　　　　　　　　　　○ Ⓕ bring you straight to city hall.

[注意] 辞典に take you to city hall nonstop が出ているが，いくつかの駅に停車する directly, straight と違って停車する駅がないことになるので同じではない。

12「車両」
(a) **乗る車両を述べる場合**
(後ろから2両目に乗っています)
I'll be in the second car ◎ Ⓐ from the last.
　　　　　　　　　　　　○ Ⓑ from the end.
　　　　　　　　　　　　△ Ⓒ from the back.

(b) **乗っている車両を尋ねるとき**
(何両目に乗っていますか)
☆ Ⓐ Which car're you going to be in?
◎ Ⓑ What car're you going to be in?
○ Ⓒ Which car're you going to be on?
○ Ⓓ What number car're you in?

第15章　交通機関に関する表現

13「下がる階段」
　　（荻窪駅で降りたら下がる階段を利用して下さい）
　　When you get off at Ogikubo Station, take the stairs
　　　　☆ Ⓐ down.
　　　　◎ Ⓑ going down.
　　　　◎ Ⓒ that go down.

14「上る階段」
　　（荻窪駅で降りたら必ず上る階段を利用して下さい）
　　When you get off at Ogikubo Station, be sure to take the stairs
　　　　☆ Ⓐ up.
　　　　◎ Ⓑ going up.
　　　　◎ Ⓒ that go up.

15「北口の７番プラットホームの階段を上った所で」
　　（北口の７番プラットホームの階段を上った所にいて下さい）
　　◎ Please stay at the top of the stairs on Platform 7 at the North exit.

16「９番プラットホームの階段を降りた所で」
　　（９番プラットホームの階段を降りた所で会いましょう）
　　Let's meet ◎ Ⓐ at the bottom of the stairs on Platform 9.
　　　　　　　　◎ Ⓑ by the stairs on Platform 9.

17「南口の改札で」
　　（南口の改札で会いましょう）
　　Let's meet ☆ Ⓐ at the South exit ticket gate.
　　　　　　　　◎ Ⓑ at the ticket gate at the South exit.
　　　　　　　　○ Ⓒ at the gate of the South exit.

18「タクシーで帰る」
　　（タクシーで帰りましょう）
　　Let's ☆ Ⓐ take a cab home.
　　　　　◎ Ⓑ take a taxi home.
　　　　　○ Ⓒ go home by cab.
　　　　　○ Ⓓ go home by taxi.

19「飛行機で帰る」

(a) 航空会社名を述べない場合
(飛行機で帰りましょう)
Let's ☆ Ⓐ fly back.
　　　 ◎ Ⓑ take a flight back.
　　　 ◎ Ⓒ catch a flight back.
　　　 ◎ Ⓓ take a plane back.
　　　 ○ Ⓔ catch a plane back.

(b) 航空会社名を述べる場合
(デルタで帰りましょう)
Let's ☆ Ⓐ go back on Delta.
　　　 ◎ Ⓑ take Delta back.
　　　 ◎ Ⓒ fly back on Delta.
　　　 ◎ Ⓓ fly on Delta back.
　　　 ○ Ⓔ travel back on Delta.
　　　 △ Ⓕ fly Delta back.

20 「通路側の席」
(通路側の席にしてくれますか)
　☆ Ⓐ Can I get an aisle seat?
　◎ Ⓑ Can I have an aisle seat?
　◎ Ⓒ Can you give me an aisle seat?
　◎ Ⓓ Is an aisle seat available?
［注意］(1)「窓側の席」は window seat.
(2) 飛行機のみならず映画館，コンサートホールなどにも使える。

21 「前のほうの席」
(前のほうの席にしてくれますか)
　☆ Ⓐ Can I get a seat in the front (row)?
　◎ Ⓑ Can I have a seat in the front (row)?
　◎ Ⓒ Can I sit in the front?
　◎ Ⓓ Can you give me a seat in the front?
　◎ Ⓔ Is a seat in the front (row) available?

22 「収容能力の席」
(この飛行機はいくつ席があるのですか)
　◎ Ⓐ How many seats does this plane have?

第15章　交通機関に関する表現

◎ Ⓑ How many passengers can ［does］ this plane hold?
○ Ⓒ How many passengers can ［does］ this plane take?
○ Ⓓ How many passengers can ［does］ this plane carry?
○ Ⓔ What's the seating capacity of this plane?
△ Ⓕ How many passengers can ［does］ this plane accommodate?

23「(飛行機)…まわり（経由）の」
　（私はサンフランシスコまわりの７時30分の飛行機で行きます）
　I'll take the 7:30 flight ☆ Ⓐ that stops at San Francisco.
　　　　　　　　　　　　　☆ Ⓑ that stops in ...
　　　　　　　　　　　　　◎ Ⓒ through ...
　　　　　　　　　　　　　△ Ⓓ by way of ...
　　　　　　　　　　　　　△ Ⓔ via ...
［**注意**］電車と飛行機では少し表現が違う。

第16章 健康・病気に関する表現

1 「健康です」
（父は健康です）
☆ Ⓐ My father's healthy.
◎ Ⓑ My father's in good health.
△ Ⓒ My father enjoys good health.
△ Ⓓ My father has good health.
× Ⓔ My father's well.
［注意］Ⓔは健康状態を尋ねられたときの答としてなら非常によく使われている。

2 「健康がすぐれない」
（彼女は健康がすぐれないんです）
☆ Ⓐ She's sick.
☆ Ⓑ She isn't healthy.
◎ Ⓒ She isn't in good health.
◎ Ⓓ She's in bad health.
◎ Ⓔ She's in poor health.

3 「健康によい」
（速歩することは健康に非常にいいです）
Walking fast's really good for ☆ Ⓐ your health.
　　　　　　　　　　　　　　 ◎ Ⓑ our health.
　　　　　　　　　　　　　　 ○ Ⓒ one's health.
　　　　　　　　　　　　　　 ○ Ⓓ the health.

4 「健康そのものに見える」
(彼は健康そのものに見えます)
He ◎ Ⓐ looks really healthy.
　　◎ Ⓑ really looks healthy.
　　○ Ⓒ looks like a really healthy guy.
　　△ Ⓓ looks like the picture of health.
[注意] 辞典に He looks like the epitome of health. が出ているが使われていない。

5 「健康によくない」
(タバコは健康によくありません)
☆ Ⓐ Smoking's bad for you.
☆ Ⓑ Smoking's bad for your health.
☆ Ⓒ Smoking can kill you.
◎ Ⓓ Smoking'll ruin your health.
○ Ⓔ Smoking hurts you.
△ Ⓕ Smoking can damage your health.
△ Ⓖ Smoking hurts your health.
△ Ⓗ Smoking kills you.
△ Ⓘ Smoking's harmful for [to] your health.

6 「寿命を縮める」
(肥満は寿命を縮めます)
☆ Ⓐ Obesity'll kill you.
☆ Ⓑ Obesity kills you.
◎ Ⓒ Obesity'll take years off your life.
◎ Ⓓ Obesity'll shorten your life span.
◎ Ⓔ Obesity'll shorten your life.
◎ Ⓕ Obesity'll make you die younger.
○ Ⓖ Obesity'll cut years off your life.
[注意] ⒸⒹⒺⒻⒼの will を取り現在形で述べてもよく使われている。またⒶⒷⒸⒹⒺⒻⒼに can を使ってもよい。

7 「病気」
(a) **一般的に言う場合**
(父は病気なんです)

◎ Ⓐ My father's sick.
◎ Ⓑ My father's ill.
◎ Ⓒ My father's feeling ill.
○ Ⓓ My father's feeling sick.
○ Ⓔ My father feels ill [sick].
[注意] ill のほうが sick より重い響きがある。

(b) 重い病気の場合
(父は重い病気なんです)
My father's ◎ Ⓐ seriously ill.
　　　　　　 ◎ Ⓑ very sick.
　　　　　　 △ Ⓒ very ill.
　　　　　　 △ Ⓓ seriously sick.

8 「危険な（病状）」
(ボブの容態は危険なんです)
Bob's in ◎ Ⓐ critical condition.
　　　　　 × Ⓑ dangerous condition.

9 「治る」
(a) 重病・重傷の場合
(父は心臓発作から回復したばかりです)
My father's just ◎ Ⓐ recovered from a heart attack.
　　　　　　　　　 ○ Ⓑ gotten over a heart attack.
　　　　　　　　　 △ Ⓒ recuperated [overcome] from a heart attack.
　　　　　　　　　 × Ⓓ gotten rid of a heart attack.

(b) 軽い病気・けがの場合
(ビルの風邪は治りましたか)
☆ Ⓐ Is Bill over his cold yet?
◎ Ⓑ Is Bill's cold better yet?
◎ Ⓒ Is Bill's cold gone yet?
◎ Ⓓ Did Bill get rid of his cold?
◎ Ⓔ Has Bill gotten his cold yet?
◎ Ⓕ Has Bill's cold gone away yet?
△ Ⓖ Has Bill gotten rid of his cold?
× Ⓗ Has Bill thrown off [recovered from, gotten well of] his cold?

第16章 健康・病気に関する表現

10「(病気が) 流行している」
(インフルエンザが流行しています)
☆ Ⓐ Everybody's getting the flu.
☆ Ⓑ The flu's really going around.
◎ Ⓒ The flu's really widespread.
○ Ⓓ The flu's really raging.
△ Ⓔ The flu's really rampant.
[注意] 辞典に prevailing, prevalent が出ているが，会話では使われていない。

11「長く持たない」
(ボブはあまり長く持たないでしょう)
Bob won't ☆ Ⓐ live much longer.
　　　　　 ◎ Ⓑ last much longer.
　　　　　 ○ Ⓒ survive much longer.

12「(病気で) やつれた」
(お母さんは病気でやつれた顔をしている)
Mom looks ☆ Ⓐ tired from her illness.
　　　　　 ☆ Ⓑ worn-out from her illness.
　　　　　 ◎ Ⓒ haggard from her illness.
　　　　　 ○ Ⓓ gaunt [worn] from her illness.
　　　　　 △ Ⓔ wasted [emaciated] from her illness.

13「視力」
(a) **正常**
(私の視力は正常です)
☆ Ⓐ I have normal eyesight.
◎ Ⓑ My eyesight's normal.
○ Ⓒ I have a normal vision.

(b) **視力は1.0**
(私の視力は1.0です)
◎ Ⓐ I have perfect vision.
◎ Ⓑ I have 20/20 vision.
◎ Ⓒ I have perfect eyesight.

◎ Ⓓ My eyesight's 20/20.
　　　◎ Ⓔ My vision's 20/20.
　　［注意］20/15は日本の1.2に相当する。

(c) 近眼
　　（彼は近眼なんです）
　　He's ◎ Ⓐ nearsighted.
　　　　 △ Ⓑ shortsighted.
　　［注意］(1) Ⓑは「近視眼的なものの見方をしている」の意味では非常によく使われている。
　　(2) 近眼は20/25以上である。

(d) 遠視
　　（彼は遠視なんです）
　　◎ He's farsighted.
　　［注意］farsighted は「長期的な視野を持っている」の意味でも非常によく使われている。

14 「(視力) 目が悪い」
　　（デイヴィッドは目が悪いんです）
　　☆ Ⓐ David has bad eyesight.
　　☆ Ⓑ David's eyesight's bad.
　　◎ Ⓒ David has bad vision.
　　○ Ⓓ David has poor vision.
　　○ Ⓔ David has poor eyesight.
　　○ Ⓕ David's sight's bad.

15 「気分がよくない」
　　（私は気分がよくないんです）
　　☆ Ⓐ I'm not feeling well.
　　☆ Ⓑ I'm not feeling good.
　　◎ Ⓒ I don't feel well.
　　◎ Ⓓ I don't feel good.
　　○ Ⓔ I'm not feeling OK.
　　［注意］辞典に I don't feel fine. I'm feeling unwell. が出ているが使用頻度は低い。

第16章 健康・病気に関する表現

16「(顔色が悪い人に) どうしたの」
(どうしたの)
What's ◎ Ⓐ wrong?
　　　　◎ Ⓑ the matter?
　　　　◎ Ⓒ the problem?

17「(健康上) 気をつける」
(風邪をひかないように気をつけて下さい)
Please ◎ Ⓐ be careful not to catch a cold.
　　　　△ Ⓑ take care not to catch a cold.
　　　　× Ⓒ watch not to catch a cold.

18「ふらふらする」
(熱が少しあって、頭がふらふらするんです)
I have a slight fever. ◎ Ⓐ My head's spinning.
　　　　　　　　　　　◎ Ⓑ I feel dizzy.
　　　　　　　　　　　○ Ⓒ My head's swimming.

19「熱が高い」
(リンダは熱が高いんです)
☆ Ⓐ Linda has a high fever.
◎ Ⓑ Linda's running a high fever.
◎ Ⓒ Linda has a high temperature.
○ Ⓓ Linda's running a high temperature.

20「…度の熱がある」
(リンダは104度の熱があるんです)
Linda has ◎ Ⓐ a fever of 104.
　　　　　 ○ Ⓑ a temperature of 104.

21「微熱がある」
(リンダは微熱があるんです)
☆ Ⓐ Linda has a slight fever.
◎ Ⓑ Linda's running a slight fever.
◎ Ⓒ Linda has a slight temperature.
◎ Ⓓ Linda's running a slight temperature.
◎ Ⓔ Linda's feeling a little feverish.

◎ Ⓕ Linda's a little feverish.

22 「熱が出る」
(リンダは今日の午後熱が出るでしょう)
◎ Ⓐ Linda'll get [run, develop, have] a high fever this afternoon.
◎ Ⓑ Linda'll be getting [running, developing] a high fever ...
◎ Ⓒ Linda'll get [run, develop, have, come down with] a high temperature ...
◎ Ⓓ Linda'll be getting [running, developing] a high temperature ...

23 「熱は何度」
(リンダの熱は何度あるの)
☆ Ⓐ How high's Linda's fever?
◎ Ⓑ How high's Linda's temperature?
◎ Ⓒ What's Linda's temperature?

[注意] (1) 上の文は家族のような間柄の話。病院の職員の間でのときはⒷが1番よく使われている。
(2) 上の文はリンダが病気で熱が高い状態のときの会話である。平熱に下がっているときはⒸを使う。
(3) 辞典に What's Linda's fever? が出ているが使われていない。

24 「鼻が詰まっている」
(私は鼻が詰まっているんです)
☆ Ⓐ I have a stuffy nose.
☆ Ⓑ My nose is stuffy.
◯ Ⓒ My nose is stuffed.
◯ Ⓓ My nose is stopped up.
◯ Ⓔ I have a stuffed up nose.
△ Ⓕ I have a stuffed nose.

[注意] 辞典に have a stopped, one's nose is stopped が出ているが使われていない。

25 「鼻水」
(私は鼻水が出るんです)
◎ Ⓐ I have a runny nose.
◎ Ⓑ My nose is running.

○ Ⓒ My nose is runny.

26 「咳がひどいんです」
(彼女は咳がひどいんです)
☆ Ⓐ She has a bad cough.
☆ Ⓑ She coughs a lot.
◎ Ⓒ She really coughs.
△ Ⓓ She coughs bad.
△ Ⓔ She coughs badly.
［注意］ⒹⒺが辞典に出ているがときどき使われる程度。

27 「ひどい咳をしていました」
(彼女はひどい咳をしていました)
She was coughing ☆ Ⓐ really bad.
　　　　　　　　◎ Ⓑ really badly.
　　　　　　　　◎ Ⓒ a lot.
　　　　　　　　△ Ⓓ very much.

28 「(健康上の) どきどきする」
(彼は心臓がどきどきしているんです)
His heart's ◎ Ⓐ pounding.
　　　　　◎ Ⓑ beating fast.
　　　　　○ Ⓒ racing.
　　　　　△ Ⓓ pounding fast.
［注意］どきどきしている速さの点ではⒸが1番、Ⓑが2番、Ⓓが3番、Ⓐが4番。

29 「アルツハイマー病」
(アレックスはアルツハイマー病なんです)
☆ Ⓐ Alex has Alzheimer's.
◎ Ⓑ Alex has Alzheimer's disease.
○ Ⓒ Alex's suffering from Alzheimer's disease.
× Ⓓ Alex has AD.
× Ⓔ Alex's suffering from AD.
［注意］辞典にⒹⒺが出ているが使われていない。

30 「胃潰瘍」

(ジョンは胃潰瘍なんです)
Jon has ◎ Ⓐ an ulcer.
　　　　　○ Ⓑ a stomach ulcer.
　　　　　△ Ⓒ a gastric ulcer.

31 「おたふく風邪」
(ティムはおたふく風邪なんです)
◎ Ⓐ Tim has the mumps.
○ Ⓑ Tim's suffering from the mumps.
× Ⓒ Tim has (infectious) parotitis.

32 「風邪」
(a) 風邪をひいている
●主語が単数のとき
(ジェフは今風邪をひいています)
◎ Jeff has a cold now.
●主語が単数で2回以上のとき
(ジェフはよく風邪をひいています)
Jeff always has ◎ Ⓐ a cold.
　　　　　　　　 ▽ Ⓑ colds.
●主語が複数のとき
(ジュリアとジェーンは風邪をひいています)
Julia and Jane have ◎ Ⓐ colds.
　　　　　　　　　　 △ Ⓑ a cold.
●鼻風邪
(アレックスは鼻風邪をひいているんです)
Alex has ◎ Ⓐ a head cold.
　　　　　△ Ⓑ a cold in the head.
[注意] 辞典に a cold on the head, a cold in the nose が出ているが使われていない。
●軽い風邪
(クリスは軽い風邪をひいているんです)
Chris has ◎ Ⓐ a mild cold.
　　　　　 ○ Ⓑ a slight cold.
●ひどい風邪
(アンはひどい風邪をひいているんです)
Ann has ◎ Ⓐ a bad [nasty] cold.

　　　　　　　○ Ⓑ a miserable cold.
●しつこいせき風邪
(マークはしつこいせき風邪をひいているんです)
Mark has ◎ Ⓐ a cough that (just) won't go away.
　　　　　　○ Ⓑ a stubborn [persistent] cough.

(b) 風邪をひく
(風邪をひかないように気をつけて下さい)
Be careful not to ☆ Ⓐ catch a cold.
　　　　　　　◎ Ⓑ come down with a cold.
　　　　　　　○ Ⓒ get a cold.
　　　　　　　○ Ⓓ catch cold.
［注意］辞典に contract [take] a cold が出ているが使われていない。

(c) 風邪をひきやすい
(アンは風邪をひきやすいんです)
　☆ Ⓐ Ann catches colds easy.
　◎ Ⓑ Ann catches a cold [colds] easily.
　△ Ⓒ Ann's likely to catch colds.
　△ Ⓓ Ann's prone [subject, susceptible] to catching colds.
　△ Ⓔ Ann's likely [prone] to catch a cold.
　△ Ⓕ Ann's susceptible [prone, subject] to catching a cold.
　△ Ⓖ Ann's susceptible to colds.
［注意］susceptible, subject は医師の間ではよく使われている。

(d) 風邪をひき直す
(ティムは風邪をひき直したんです)
Tim caught ◎ Ⓐ another cold.
　　　　　○ Ⓑ a cold again.
　　　　　× Ⓒ cold again.
　　　　　× Ⓓ a fresh cold.
［注意］ⒸⒹが多くの辞典に出ているが使われていない。

33 「かっけ」
(グレッグはかっけなんです)
　☆ Ⓐ Greg has beriberi.
　◎ Ⓑ Greg's suffering from beriberi.

△ ⓒ Greg's suffering beriberi.

34 「肝硬変」
(クレイは肝硬変なんです)
☆ Ⓐ Clay has cirrhosis of the liver.
◎ Ⓑ Clay's suffering from cirrhosis of the liver.
△ ⓒ Clya's suffering of cirrhosis of the liver.
× Ⓓ Clay's suffering liver cirrhosis.
[注意] Ⓓが辞典に出ているが使われていない。

35 「下痢」
(ジミーは昨日から下痢をしているんです)
Jimmy's had ◎ Ⓐ diarrhea since yesterday.
　　　　　　× Ⓑ loose bowels ...
[注意] Ⓑが辞典に出ているが使われていない。

36 「後天性白内障」
(a)　左(右)の目
(彼は左の目が後天性白内障なんです)
◎ Ⓐ He has cataract in his left eye.
△ Ⓑ He's suffering from cataract ...
[注意] 辞典に have acquired ［congenital］ cataract が出ているが使われていない。

(b)　両目
(彼は後天性白内障なんです)
◎ Ⓐ He has cataracts.
○ Ⓑ He has cataracts in his eyes.
△ ⓒ He's suffering from cataracts.

37 「コレラ」
(スィンディはコレラなんです)
◎ Ⓐ Cindy has cholera.
○ Ⓑ Cindy's suffering from cholera.

38 「痔」
(トムは痔なんです)

第16章 健康・病気に関する表現

◎ Ⓐ Tom has hemorrhoids.
○ Ⓑ Tom's suffering from hemorrhoids.
× Ⓒ Tom has piles.
× Ⓓ Tom has speed bump.
［注意］辞典にⒸⒹが出ているが使われていない。

39 「持病がありますか」
（あなたは持病がありますか）
☆ Ⓐ Do you have any health problems?
◎ Ⓑ Do you have any problems with your health?
◎ Ⓒ Do you have a problem with your health?
◎ Ⓓ Do you have any trouble with your health?
◎ Ⓔ Is there anything wrong with your health problem?
◎ Ⓕ Do you have any health trouble?

40 「しょう紅熱」
（ジュリーはしょう紅熱です）
◎ Ⓐ Julie has scarlet fever.
○ Ⓑ Julie's suffering from scarlet fever.

41 「小児麻痺」
（私の息子は小児麻痺なんです）
◎ Ⓐ He has polio.
○ Ⓑ He's suffering from polio.
△ Ⓒ He has infantile paralysis.
［注意］辞典に be suffering from infantile paralysis が出ているが使われていない。

42 「食中毒」
（デイヴィッドは食中毒です）
☆ Ⓐ David has food poisoning.
◎ Ⓑ David's suffering from food poisoning.
○ Ⓒ David's suffering food poisoning.

43 「心臓が悪い」
（彼は心臓が悪いんです）
☆ Ⓐ He has a heart problem.

◎ Ⓑ He has a heart condition.
◎ Ⓒ He has heart trouble.
◯ Ⓓ He has trouble with his heart.
◯ Ⓔ He has a problem with his heart.

44「心不全」
(父は心不全を起こしているんです)
My father's ☆ Ⓐ having a stroke.
　　　　　　◎ Ⓑ suffering from a stroke.
　　　　　　◯ Ⓒ having [suffering from] heart failure.
　　　　　　✕ Ⓓ having a heart stroke.

45「喘息」
(父は喘息なんです)
◎ Ⓐ My father has asthma.
◯ Ⓑ My father's suffering from asthma.

46「中耳炎」
(彼は中耳炎なんです)
◎ Ⓐ He has a middle-ear infection.
◯ Ⓑ He's suffering from infection.
◯ Ⓒ His middle-ear's infected.
◯ Ⓓ He has a middle-ear inflammation.
△ Ⓔ He has otitis media.

47「腸チフス」
(スーザンは腸チフスなんです)
◎ Ⓐ Susan has typhoid fever.
◯ Ⓑ Susan's suffering from typhoid fever.

48「腸閉塞」
(彼は腸閉塞なんです)
☆ Ⓐ He has an intestinal blockage.
◎ Ⓑ His intestines're blocked.
◯ Ⓒ He has an intestinal obstruction.
◯ Ⓓ He has a blockage in his intestines.

第16章　健康・病気に関する表現

49「てんかん」
（彼はてんかんなんです）
☆ Ⓐ He has epilepsy.
◎ Ⓑ He has epileptic seizures.
○ Ⓒ He has epileptic fits.
○ Ⓓ He's suffering from epileptic seizures.
○ Ⓔ He's suffering from epileptic fits.

50「点滴を受ける」
●受けている状態を述べるとき
（患者は点滴を受けています）
The patient's ◎ Ⓐ on an IV.
　　　　　　△ Ⓑ getting an intravenous drip.
●医者に依頼するとき
（点滴を受けたいのですが）
◎ Ⓐ Will you give me an IV?
◎ Ⓑ Can I get an IV?
× Ⓒ Can I get a DIV?
[注意] 日本の病院内ではDIVと言っているが，英語では使われていない。

51「肉離れ」
（ロンは肉離れを起こしているんです）
◎ Ⓐ Ron has a pulled muscle.
△ Ⓑ Ron's suffering from a pulled muscle.

52「肺炎」
（キャスィーは肺炎なんです）
☆ Ⓐ Cathy has pneumonia.
◎ Ⓑ Cathy's suffering from pneumonia.
○ Ⓒ Cathy has inflammation of the lung.

53「梅毒」
（アレックスは梅毒なんです）
◎ Ⓐ Alex has syphilis.
○ Ⓑ Alex's suffering from syphilis.
× Ⓒ Alex's syphilitic.
[注意] Ⓒが辞典に出ているが使われていない。

54「肺病」
　　（ジャックは肺病なんです）
　　☆ Ⓐ Jack has TB.
　　◎ Ⓑ Jack's suffering from TB.
　　○ Ⓒ Jack has tuberculosis.
　　○ Ⓓ Jack's suffering from tuberculosis.
　　× Ⓔ Jack has consumption.
　　［注意］辞典にⒺが出ているが今は使われていない。

55「白血病」
　　（ボブは白血病なんです）
　　◎ Ⓐ Bob has leukemia.
　　○ Ⓑ Bob suffering from leukemia.

56「膀胱炎」
　　（彼は膀胱炎なんです）
　　☆ Ⓐ He has a bladder infection.
　　○ Ⓑ He's suffering from a bladder infection.
　　△ Ⓒ He has an inflammation of the bladder.
　　△ Ⓓ He has an inflamed bladder.
　　△ Ⓔ He has cystitis.
　　［注意］Ⓔは医者の間では非常によく使われている。

57「不眠症」
　　（父は不眠症なんです）
　　☆ Ⓐ My father has insomnia.
　　◎ Ⓑ My father's an insomniac.
　　◎ Ⓒ My father can't sleep [get to sleep].
　　◎ Ⓓ My father's having trouble [a hard time, a problem] sleeping.
　　◎ Ⓔ My father has trouble [a hard time] sleeping.
　　○ Ⓕ My father can't fall asleep.
　　○ Ⓖ My father's suffering from insomnia [a sleeping disorder].

58「流感」
　　（ジェフは流感にかかっているんです）
　　☆ Ⓐ Jeff has the flu.

第16章　健康・病気に関する表現

○ Ⓑ Jeff's suffering from the flu.

59「淋病」
（スティーヴは淋病なんです）
◎ Ⓐ Steve has gonorrhea.
○ Ⓑ Steve's suffering from gonorrhea.

60「けがをする」
(a) 事故の場合
（リズは昨夜車の事故でけがをしたんです）
Liz ☆ Ⓐ got hurt in a car crash last night.
　　☆ Ⓑ was hurt ...
　　◎ Ⓒ got injured ...
　　◎ Ⓓ was injured ...
　　○ Ⓔ was wounded ...
　　△ Ⓕ got wounded ...
［注意］テレビ，新聞などのニュース英語ではⒷⒹⒺが非常によく使われている。

(b) 凶器が使われた場合
（サリーは強盗にナイフで刺されてけがをしたんです）
Sally ☆ Ⓐ was hurt by a robber with a knife.
　　　☆ Ⓑ got hurt ...
　　　◎ Ⓒ was wounded ...
　　　◎ Ⓓ got wounded ...
　　　△ Ⓔ was injured ...
　　　△ Ⓕ got injured ...
［注意］(1) テレビ，新聞などのニュース英語ではⒸⒺが１番よく使われている。
(2) 辞典に① be wounded は故意に，② be hurt, ③ be injured は非故意に「けがをさせられた」ときに使い分けられていると出ているが，これらは英語の慣用事実を歪曲している。①②③のいずれを使うかは話し手の主観による。He was ① wounded ［② hurt, ③ injured］because his wife stabbed him with a knife. （彼は妻がナイフで刺したからけがをしたんです）出血の量が多かったと話し手が思えば①，多くなかったという気持ちで述べるときは②，③は②の改まった表現。血を見ることに慣れていない人，感受性の強い人は出血の量が少なくても①を使う。

[187]

(c) 重傷を負った場合
   (ローズは強盗にナイフで重傷を負わされたんです)
   Rose ☆ Ⓐ was badly [seriously] hurt by a robber with a knife.
        ☆ Ⓑ got badly hurt ...
        ◎ Ⓒ got seriously hurt ...
        ◎ Ⓓ was badly [seriously] wounded ...
        ◎ Ⓔ got badly [seriously] wounded ...
        △ Ⓕ was badly [seriously] injured ...
        △ Ⓖ got badly [seriously] injured ...

(d) 主人公の不注意の場合
   (ビルはナイフでけがをしたんです)
   Bill ◎ Ⓐ hurt himself with a knife.
        ○ Ⓑ wounded ...
        △ Ⓒ injured ...

61 「痛い」

(a) 頭痛
   ●頭全体に痛みがあるとき
   (私は昨日頭が痛かったんです)
   ◎ Ⓐ I had a headache yesterday.
   ◎ Ⓑ My head hurt ...
   ○ Ⓒ My head was hurting [aching] ...
   ○ Ⓓ My head ached ...
   △ Ⓔ My head was painful ...
   [注意] (1) 辞典に My head smarted yesterday. が出ているが使われていない。
   (2) 上の表現は stomachache（腹痛）, toothache（歯痛）, backache（背中の痛み）, earache（耳の痛み）に使っても使用頻度は同じ。

   ●頭全体に強い痛みがあるとき
   (私は昨日すごく頭が痛かったんです)
   ☆ Ⓐ My head was killing me yesterday.
   ☆ Ⓑ I had a terrible headache ...
   ◎ Ⓒ I had a severe headache ...
   ◎ Ⓓ I had an awful headache ...
   ◎ Ⓔ I had a horrible headache ...

第16章　健康・病気に関する表現

◎ Ⓕ I had a bad headache ...
◎ Ⓖ My head really hurt ...
○ Ⓗ My head was really hurting ...
○ Ⓘ My head really ached ...
△ Ⓙ My head was really aching ...

[注意] (1) Ⓐが1番強く，Ⓒが2番，ⒷⒹⒺが3番，ⒻⒼⒽが4番，ⒾⒿが1番弱い。
(2) 上の表現は stomachache (腹痛), toothache (歯痛), backache (背中の痛み), earache (耳の痛み) に使っても使用頻度は同じ。

●頭の一部または一点がすごく痛いとき
(私は頭の右側がすごく痛いんです)

☆ Ⓐ I have a terrible pain on the right side of my head.
◎ Ⓑ I have a lot of pain on the right side of my head.
◎ Ⓒ I have an awful [a sharp, a bad] pain on the right side of my head.
◎ Ⓓ The right side of my head really hurts.
◎ Ⓔ The right side of my head's really hurting (me).
◎ Ⓕ The right side of my head hurts terribly [a lot, bad].
○ Ⓖ The right side of my head hurts badly.
△ Ⓗ The right side of my head hurts awfully.
△ Ⓘ The right side of my head's really painful.

[注意] (1) Ⓐ〜Ⓒは頭の内部が病気，または打撲で痛いとき。
(2) Ⓓ〜Ⓘは頭の内部か表面か不明だが，原因はⒶ〜Ⓒと同じで病気，または打撲で痛いとき。

●がんがんする痛み
(私は昨日頭ががんがん痛かったんです)

☆ Ⓐ My head was really killing me yesterday.
☆ Ⓑ My head was pounding ...
☆ Ⓒ I had a pounding headache ...
◎ Ⓓ I had a throbbing headache ...
◎ Ⓔ My head was throbbing ...
○ Ⓕ My head throbbed ...
△ Ⓖ My head pounded ...

[注意] 辞典に be stinging が出ているが使われていない。

[189]

(b) 目
　●普通に述べるとき
　（昨日私は目が痛かったんです）
　☆ Ⓐ My eyes hurt yesterday.
　◎ Ⓑ My eyes were sore ...
　○ Ⓒ My eyes were hurting ...
　○ Ⓓ I had sore eyes ...

　●強い痛みがあったとき
　（昨日私は目がすごく痛かったんです）
　☆ Ⓐ My eyes really hurt yesterday.
　◎ Ⓑ My eyes hurt a lot ...
　◎ Ⓒ My eyes were really sore ...
　◎ Ⓓ My eyes were really hurting ...
　◎ Ⓔ My eyes really bothered me ...
　○ Ⓕ I had really sore eyes ...
　○ Ⓖ My eyes were really killing me ...
　○ Ⓗ My eyes hurt terribly ...
　○ Ⓘ My eyes hurt horribly ...
　○ Ⓙ My eyes hurt awfully ...

　●ちくちくする（ひりひりする）痛みがあったとき
　（昨日私の目はちくちく痛かったんです）
　My eyes ◎ Ⓐ were really burning yesterday.
　　　　　　 ◎ Ⓑ really burned ...
　　　　　　 ◎ Ⓒ were really stinging ...
　　　　　　 ◎ Ⓓ really stung ...

(c) のど
　●普通に述べるとき
　（私は昨日のどが痛かったんです）
　◎ Ⓐ I had a scratchy throat yesterday.
　◎ Ⓑ My throat was scratchy ...
　◎ Ⓒ I had a sore throat ...
　◎ Ⓓ My throat was sore ...
　◎ Ⓔ My throat hurt ...
　◎ Ⓕ My throat was hurting ...

第16章　健康・病気に関する表現

[注意] ⒶⒷは初期，ⒸⒹはⒶⒷより悪化している。ⒺⒻはいずれの段階でも使える。

●強い痛みがあったとき
（私は昨日のどがとても痛かったんです）
◎ Ⓐ I had a really [very] scratchy throat yesterday.
◎ Ⓑ My throat was really [very] scratchy ...
◎ Ⓒ I had a really [very] sore throat ...
◎ Ⓓ My throat was really [very] sore ...
◎ Ⓔ My throat was really hurting ...
◎ Ⓕ My throat really hurt ...
◎ Ⓖ My throat hurt a lot ...
◎ Ⓗ My throat was hurting a lot ...
○ Ⓘ My throat hurt terribly [awfully, horribly] ...
○ Ⓙ I had a lot of pain in my throat ...
[注意] Ⓘが1番悪化している状態。

INDEX

【あ】

愛妻家	114
あいさつ	1
朝のあいさつ	1
午後のあいさつ	1
夜のあいさつ	2
別れるとき	2
思いがけなく知人・友人に出会ったとき	3
思いがけない場所で知人・友人に会ったとき	3
意味なく相手の健康を尋ねるとき	3
愛している	108
（親・兄弟・姉妹・子供へ）愛している	33
愛着がある	33
会う	8
知り合うとき	8
知り合うプロセスがあるとき	8
約束して友人，知人，ビジネス上人と会うとき	8
約束して場所を明示して会うとき	8
会う日時，曜日を明示するとき	9
偶然会うとき	9
明るい人	53
あくせくする	123
仕事に対する姿勢を述べるとき	123
問題に対する姿勢を述べるとき	123
生き方，暮らし方のような人生観を述べるとき	123
頭にくる	37
熱い仲だ	110
厚かましい	50
暑くてやりきれない	17
暑くなる	16
アパート	126
住んでいることを述べるとき	126
ビル全体を述べるとき	126
あばずれ女	117
あぶらっこい	148
料理の内容	148
料理の仕方	148
あぶらっこい	148
油で汚れた	92
手	92
髪の毛	92
甘党	146
少し否定的に述べるとき	146
強く否定的に述べるとき	146
雨がやむ	22
歩いて下さい	157
アルツハイマー病	179
（時間を）合わせる	26
一般的に述べるとき	26
進んでいた（遅れていた）ので合わせたと述べるとき	26
「（目覚ましを何時に）合わせる」と述べるとき	27

【い】

いいお天気です	15
いい男	86
身体全体の容姿の場合	86
顔の場合	86
セクシーだというニュアンスの場合	86
イージーオーダーの	100
胃潰瘍	179
意気消沈している	40
いじめる	74
深刻に	74
軽い気持で	74
異性愛者	118
急いでいません	29
急いで帰る	28
急いで連れて行く	29
急ぐ	28
目的地に言及する場合	28
命令文の場合	28
急いで何かを持ってこさせる場合	28
（車のスピードを）急ぐ	28
普通に述べる場合	29
強く述べる場合	29
痛い	188
頭痛	188

INDEX

目	190
のど	190
いただきます	138
市様模様（碁盤縞）の	106
一文無し	123
一匹狼	73
一般的に述べる場合	73
政治家	73
いやな天気	15
色が合う	96

【う】

上の階の	161
うだるように暑い	17
うぬぼれる	68
動作を表す	68
状態を表す	68
裏切る	71
うれしい	33
同僚に話す場合	33
強調して同僚に話す場合	34
浮気する	115
非難の気持が強い場合	115
非難の気持が軽い場合	116
客観的に述べる場合	116
少しうらやましい気持で述べる場合	116
浮気している相手の数が多いことを述べる場合	116
「妻には男がいるんです」と述べる場合	117

【え】

営業時間	156
塩分の多い	150
塩分が非常に多い	150

【お】

横柄な	57
大食い	145
オーダーメイドの	100
お決りですか	137
遅れる	128
毎月支払う家賃（ローン・会費）	128
遅れる	27
遅れる	30
コンサート・会合などのように動かないのに	30
飛行機・電車のような動くもの	31
怒っている	36
気分を害している	36
むっとしている	36
怒って席を立つ	36
おしゃべり	55
おたふく風邪	180
おっとりしている（のん気な）	57
お腹がぺこぺこ	143
思いやりがある	49
お持ち帰り	137

【か】

階級	124
上流階級	124
中流の上の階級	124
中流階級	125
中流の下の階級	125
下層階級	125
貧民階級から上流階級にのし上がったとき出世話として述べる	125
外向的	55
甲斐性がある	121
外食する	143
（…行きと）書いてある	167
風邪	180
風邪をひいている	180
風邪をひく	181
風邪をひきやすい	181
風邪をひき直す	181
風がごうごう吹く	23
風が強い	24
風が出てくる	23
風がひゅうひゅう吹いています	24
風がやむ	24
かっけ	181
かっとなる	36
家庭的	114
辛い	149
料理	149
チーズ	149
ドレッシング	149
ワイン	149

（顔が）可愛い	84
息子	84
娘	84
動物	84
（笑顔が）可愛い	84
可愛いくてしようがない	85
変わりやすい天気	19
肝硬変	182
看板	156
看板です（閉店です）	156
看板を出す	156

【き】

気が多い	117
着飾っている	98
聞き覚えがある	75
危険な（病状）	174
危険な	132
「危険な所」と述べる場合	132
都市・町・地域を述べる場合	133
傷つく	39
既製の	100
期待する	48
一般的に述べる場合	48
改まった言い方で述べる場合	49
北口の7番プラットホームの階段を上った所で	169
着ている	96
現在の状態	96
現在の状態として名詞を修飾している場合	97
過去の一時的状態	97
過去の習慣的内容を表す文で every day がある場合	97
過去の習慣的内容として述べるとき	97
気取っている	57
気に障る	37
気分がいいんです	34
気分がよくない	176
気分屋	57
気まずいんです	70
行儀よくする	61
子供に注意する場合	61
成人（45歳位まで）の女性が述べる場合	61
成人（45歳位まで）の男性が述べる場合	62
中年以上の女性が述べる場合	62
中年以上の男性が述べる場合	62
今日中に	32
恐怖症	51
高所恐怖症	51
女性恐怖性	51
対人恐怖症	51
閉所恐怖症	51
ホモ恐怖症	52
霧がかかる	21
霧が晴れる	21
霧が深い	21
ぎりぎりで	31
ぎりぎりの値段です	155
きれい好き	55
（契約が）切れる	128
（忍耐が）切れる	37
（健康上）気をつける	177
気をもませる	111
禁煙席にしていただけますか	135

【く】

クーラー	129
機械に言及する場合	129
稼動に言及する場合	129
崩れる	19
口先だけ	73
口やかましい	66
クツのサイズ	101
くどい	12
9番プラットホームの階段を降りた所で	169
くやしい	37
感情的に述べる場合	37
誰がくやしいのかを述べる場合	38
くやしくて	38
暮らす	120
贅沢に暮らす	120
裕福に暮らす	120
快適に暮らす	120
質素に暮らす	121
倹約して暮らす	121
生活力以上の暮らしをする	121
苦しい	122

INDEX

苦労性	57
苦労する	42
苦労したひとつの行為を述べるとき	42
一連の苦労を述べるとき	42

【け】

軽蔑する	43
怒りの気持が入っている場合	43
怒りの気持がない場合	43
けがをする	187
事故の場合	187
凶器が使われた場合	187
重傷を負った場合	188
主人公の不注意の場合	188
結婚記念日	112
結婚式	113
式のとき	113
披露宴のとき	113
結婚する	112
結婚する相手を述べる場合	112
結婚する相手を述べない場合	112
下品な言葉を使う	63
下痢	182
健康がすぐれない	172
健康そうに見える	173
健康です	172
健康によい	172
健康によくない	173

【こ】

恋しい	44
物が手に入らないとき	44
人に会えないとき	44
恋している	108
恋人	109
女性	109
男性	109
好感を持っている	69
好感を持っていない（よく思っていない）	69
高級な（住宅街）	131
2人称・3人称が主語のとき	131
1人称が主語のとき	131
高級レストラン	134
高級ワイン	138
格子柄の	106

公団	127
日本	127
アメリカ	127
後天性白内障	182
左（右）の目	182
両目	182
行動が速い	72
行動力のある人	72
コーディネート	96
「コーディネートされている」ことを述べるとき	96
「コーディネートさせる」ことを述べるとき	96
コーヒーを入れる	151
ここはどこですか	157
ここでお召し上がり，それともお持ち帰り	137
心があったかい	49
小雨が降る	21
こってりした	148
量は少ないがカロリーのある料理	149
量もカロリーもある料理	149
言葉遣い	62
この先	158
通りの数ブロック先	158
同じブロックの場合	158
「この少し先」の場合	158
「このずっと先」の場合	158
この通りの少し先	159
好みがうるさい	146
ごますり	65
下品な表現	65
下品でない表現	65
文章で使われる表現	65
コレラ	182
怖い	34
人が主語のとき	34
人が主語でないとき	34

【さ】

サービス	155
一般の店で	155
高級店で	155
財産	123
一般的に言う場合	123
「財産家」と言う場合	124

サイズ	101	努力でなく性質上	53
２まわり大きいと述べる場合	101	じゃまたね	4
サイズを述べる場合	101	車両	168
下がる階段	169	乗る車両を述べる場合	168
酒を飲むとすぐ酔っ払う	152	乗っている車両を尋ねるとき	168
酒を飲んでもすぐ酔わない	152	十字形模様の	106
支える	70	10人並み	85
精神的に	70	週末に（は）	32
士気	71	10名です	135
差し込み	129	収容能力の席	170
入れるとき	129	趣味に合わない	98
抜くとき	129	寿命を縮める	173
淋しい	45	純粋な	56
寒いです	19	紹介する	7
普通に述べるとき	19	個人に対して紹介する場合	7
強調するとき	20	大勢の人に対して紹介する場合	8
残（冷）酷な	58	少食	145
残念です	11	しょう紅熱	183
		小児麻痺	183
【し】		上品です	78
痔	182	女性	78
ジェットバスのある	130	男性	78
塩辛い	150	食事中	147
自業自得	71	食中毒	183
…したくてたまらない	35	知り合う	9
どこかへ行きたいと述べる場合	35	初めて紹介された場合	9
人に会いたいと述べる場合	35	パーティーなどの退出時に「お知り合いに	
下の階の	161	なれてよかった」と述べる場合	10
実に嫌な（不愉快な，うんざりさせられる）	50	尻に敷かれている	114
失礼です	60	視力	175
一般的に述べる場合	60	正常	175
強調して述べる場合	60	視力は1.0	175
支払う	140	近眼	176
主語が１人称の場合	140	遠視	176
主語が２人称の場合	140	しわ	87
持病がありますか	183	しわ	103
脂肪の少ない	147	衣服	103
脂肪のない	147	生地	104
しま模様の	105	生地と折り目	104
一般的に言う場合	105	折り目	104
太いしま模様の	106	信号	157
細いしま模様の	106	心臓が悪い	183
社交的ではない	54	心配させる	45
社交的な	53	心配性	46
努力するニュアンスの場合	53	心配する	45

[196]

INDEX

命令文のとき	45	
状態として述べるとき	45	
待ち遠しいというニュアンスがあるとき		
	45	
心不全	184	

【す】
数軒先	158
ずうずうしい	50
すぐ上の階の	161
（天気が）すぐ変わる	19
すぐ下の階の	161
すぐそばに	160
（…の）直向いに	160
すごい	12
少し手前	159
ずけずけ言う	58
進む	27
（時計が）進んでいる	27
「…分進んでいる」と述べる場合	27
「何分進んでいる」と述べる場合	27
（遅れている時計を）進める	27
すっぱい	150
すみません	4
謝罪する内容に言及しない場合	5
今現在相手に迷惑をかけている内容に言及して謝罪する場合	5
迷惑の内容が現在完了の継続内容の場合	5
すらっとしている	79
女性の場合	79
男性の場合	79
スラム街	132
一般的なスラム街	132
特定の少数民族が住んでいるスラム街	132
（生地が）すり切れる	103
ずるい	49

【せ】
生活水準	122
維持を述べる場合	122
高いことを述べる場合	122
生活費	122
席	136
席がある	136
咳がひどいんです	179

席に座らせてくれる	137
席を取っておく	136
席を替わる	137
セックスアピール	79
「ある」と述べる場合	79
「ない」と述べる場合	80
接待が上手です	54
栓	130
栓をする	130
栓を外す	130
せんさくがましい	66
喘息	184

【そ】
そっけない	67
外で食べる	143
単に外で食べることを述べるとき	143
昼食とか夕食に言及するとき	143
その日暮らしをしている	121
そばに	160
そばを	160
空模様からすると	18
尊敬する	42
普通に述べる場合	43
「非常に尊敬している」と述べる場合	43

【た】
大事にする	111
体重を減らす	82
一般的に述べるとき	82
下腹部のぜい肉を頭に置いて述べるとき	82
タクシーで帰る	169
楽しむ	41
クラシックコンサートのような知的な所へ行った場合	41
スポーツ・ピクニック・ロックコンサート	41
ハネムーンのような一生に一度という経験	42
だぶだぶした	102
ズボン	102
スーツ・上着	102
食べ過ぎ	144
食べる	142

[197]

食べ始めることを述べる場合	142
進行形の場合	142
具体的に食事することを述べる場合	142
ガツガツ食べる場合	143
だまされやすい	68
だます	67
「だます」行為を述べる場合	67
だまして何かを巻きあげる場合	67
「何に」だますかを明示して述べる場合	67
炭水化物の少ない食事	150

【ち】

中耳炎	184
昼食を作る	147
腸チフス	184
ちょうど	25
ちょうど	155
(到着の時間が) ちょうど…	26
腸閉塞	184
直行する	168
賃貸している	127
家主が	127
テナントが	127

【つ】

通路側の席	170
突き当たった所に	159
通り	159
ビルの中	160
告げ口する	65
子供の場合	65
つけ込む	68
(天候が) 続く	18
through [until] がある場合	18
for＋期間がある場合	18
非人称の It を主語にとるある種の動詞を従える場合	18
(比喩的な意味で) つまずく	117
冷たい	58
詰める	103
つやつやした髪	87
つやつやした肌	89

【て】

…で通勤する	163
電車, バスなどで	163
車で	163
帰宅の方法も言及する場合	163
でぶ	82
天候に関係なく	18
(詫びに対して) どういたしまして	5
I'm so sorry. と深く謝罪されたとき	5
Excuse me. と軽く詫びられたとき	5
てんかん	185
点滴を受ける	185
(感謝されて) どういたしまして	6
高級な店で客が礼を言ったとき	6
コンビニ・スーパーなどで客が礼を言ったとき	6
友人・家族同士などで丁重さが求められていないとき	6

【と】

(顔色が悪い人に) どうしたの	177
(約束を破ったり, 遅刻ばかりする人に対して責める気持で) どうしたんだい	11
同性愛	118
客観的に述べるとき	118
否定的に述べるとき	118
「同性愛結婚」と述べるとき	119
同棲する	112
批判的に述べる場合	112
客観的に述べる場合	112
糖分のない	150
遠ざける	71
どきどきする	108
(健康上の) どきどきする	179
土砂降り	20
途中で	162
…へ行く途中で	162
…からの帰宅途中で	162
どなた様のお名前でご予約する	140
…度の熱がある	177
(塩・コショウ・マスタードなどを) とる	151
取れかかっている	103

【な】

内向的	55
治る	174
重病・重傷の場合	174

INDEX

軽い病気・けがの場合	174
長く持たない	175
長袖のシャツ	101
仲直りする	113
(同性同士が) 仲直りする	70
長持ちする	103
長持ちする	106
仲を取り持つ	113
(悪い状態に) なる	151
なれなれしい	75
一般的に述べる場合	75
特に性的ななれなれしさを表す場合	75
何時	25
漠然と尋ねるとき	25
あなたの時計でと明示するとき	25
何とおっしゃったのですか	6
丁重に尋ねる場合	6
普通に尋ねる場合	7
乱暴に尋ねる場合	7
何番目	167
何名様	135

【に】

似合う	94
物が主語の場合	94
人が主語の場合	95
肉離れ	185
24時間ドアマンがいる	130
…に座れますか	135
(人が) 似ている	92
容姿	92
性格	93
瓜ふたつ	93
…になりそうです	20
にわか雨にあう	21

【ね】

熱が高い	177
熱が出る	178
熱は何度	178
…年振りの大雨	22

【の】

…の少し先	159
喉から手が出るほど欲しい	35

上る階段	169
(アルコール) 飲む	151
普通に述べる場合	151
強調して述べる場合	151
(このまま) 乗っていく	167
乗り換える	166
(…に) 乗り換える	166
乗り越す	167
乗る	164
命令・提案	164
乗る駅名を明示する場合	164
目的地を明示する場合	164
乗っている状態に言及する場合	164
行先を尋ねる場合	164
乗った駅名を尋ねる場合	165
「乗ったことがある」という経験を述べる場合	165
ノンオイルの	148
飲ん兵衛	152

【は】

肺炎	185
梅毒	185
肺病	186
入る	134
レストラン・店などに言及する場合	134
レストラン・店などに言及しないとき	134
激しい雷雨	22
恥ずかしい	46
失敗を見られるなどして「ばつが悪い」	46
法律に違反して	46
モラルに反したことをして	46
自分に能力がないことに対して怒りの気持で	46
おどおどしたり、はにかみ・内気の「恥ずかしがり」	47
肌が荒れている	89
肌がきれいです	89
顔	89
顔以外のとき	89
肌が黒い	88
話し手が白人の場合	88
話し手が非白人の場合	88
肌が白い	88
白人	88

非白人	88
白血病	186
八方美人	54
鼻があぐらをかいている	91
鼻が上を向いている	91
鼻がかっこいい	91
鼻が詰まっている	178
話好きの人	54
鼻水	178
花模様の	105
サイズに言及しないとき	105
サイズに言及するとき	105
晴れ上がる	15
晴れのち曇り	16
反発する	38

【ひ】

ひげ	90
本物のひげ	90
つけひげ	90
飛行機で帰る	169
航空会社名を述べない場合	170
航空会社名を述べる場合	170
久し振りです	4
昔の部下・学生・友人に会って	4
昔の上司・恩師などに会って	4
女性が男性の友人に，または女性の友人に会って	4
久し振りにいい天気	16
久し振りに飲む	152
非常階段	128
美人	85
普通に述べる場合	85
「すごい美人」と述べる場合	85
「セクシー」であるという意味の「すごい美人」	86
ぴったり	102
サイズを述べるとき	102
似合うと述べたいとき	102
ひどい咳をしていました	179
ひどい吹雪	23
人感センサーが付いている	130
人（みんな）に好かれる	70
微熱がある	177
秘密	76

「秘密を守る」と言う場合	76
「秘密を漏らす」と言う場合	76
日焼けする	87
普通に日焼けしている場合	87
非常に日焼けしている場合	87
炎症を起こしている場合	88
評価する	76
過大評価する場合	76
過小評価する場合	77
病気	173
一般的に言う場合	173
重い病気の場合	174
美容整形手術	91
目・鼻などの形を整える手術	91
しわ取りの手術	92
卑劣な	50

【ふ】

ファッションのセンスがいい	96
ぶっきらぼうな	58
太っている	81
客観的に述べる場合	81
主観的に述べる場合	81
太らないように気をつけている	83
太り気味	81
吹雪です	23
不眠症	186
ブラインドを上げる	131
ブラインドを下ろす	130
ふらふらする	177
振られる	111
分譲地	131

【へ】

（交通機関が）…へ行く	166

【ほ】

膀胱炎	186
誇りを持っている	47
自分自身に対して	47
現在の幸運・現在の状態に感謝して述べるとき	47
ずうっとやってきたことに対して	47
達成した地位に対して	48
ほめる	63

INDEX

普通に述べる場合	63
改まった調子で述べるとき	63
強めて述べている場合	64
本当ですね	10
改まった話し方をする必要がないとき	10
改まった話し方をする必要があるとき	11
本物の	146

【ま】

舞い上がっている	39
昇進・合格・成功	39
異性関係で	40
真裏に	160
前のほうの席	170
マザコン	59
まじめである	56
まだ	26
時間がたつのが早いと思ったとき	26
時間がたつのが遅いと思ったとき	26
まつ毛	90
「きれいです」と述べる場合	90
「長い」と述べる場合	90
(交通機関に) 間に合う	30
(約束に) 間に合う	30
漠然と「週末に」と言う場合	32
週末の中の「ある1日」を意味する場合	32
「毎週末」を意味する場合	32
…まわり（経由）で	168
(飛行機) …まわり（経由）の	171
マンション	126
賃借しているとき	126
高層マンション	126
ワンルームマンション	126
分譲マンション	126
満腹です	144
もうこれ以上食べられないという状態のとき	144
「単に満腹です」という状態のとき	144
「すごく満腹です」という状態のとき	145

【み】

見栄	71
見栄を張る	72
2人称のことを述べる場合	72
3人称のことを述べる場合	72
水玉の	104
普通に述べるとき	104
「大きな水玉の」と述べるとき	105
水をさす	74
人間関係	74
博士号・弁護士の資格などを取ろうとしている努力を伴う計画・夢など	74
南口の改札で	169

【む】

無口です	73
蒸し暑い	16
無地の	104
無邪気な	56
夢中です	109
10代の女性が一方的に夢中になっている場合	109
成人が一方的に夢中になっている場合	110
年齢に関係なく両者が夢中になっている場合	110
無頓着な	56
胸が詰まる	39
胸のあいた	101

【め】

目	89
大きい目	89
優しい目	89
怖い目	90
(視力) 目が悪い	176

【や】

焼く	138
焼き方を尋ねる場合	138
希望する焼き方を述べる場合	139
焼けつくように暑い	17
安い	153
品物が主語の場合	153
料金・税金のような無形物が主語の場合	153
比較級・最上級の場合	153
「いい買物」というニュアンスの「安い」	154
安くする	154

[201]

（病気で）やつれた	175
やせこけている	80
一般的に述べる場合	80
背が高くてやせていることを強調する場合	81
（人が）やせている	80
（寝不足で）やつれた	81
山の手	132

【ゆ】

優越感	48
雪がたくさん降る	22

【よ】

呼びかけ	12
女性に呼びかける場合	12
男性に呼びかける場合	13
予約	140
予約する	140
弱虫な（意気地のない）	59

【り】

リバウンドする	83
リバウンドした程度に言及しない場合	83
少し体重が増えた場合	83
完全に元に戻ってしまった場合	83
流感	186
（病気が）流行している	175
流行する	98
現在（流行しています）	98
未来（流行するでしょう）	98
大流行している	99
流行に遅れない	99
流行に振りまわされている	100
流行の先端をいく	99
流行を追う	99
両性愛者	118
料理	145
広く一般的に使う場合	145
洗練された料理を述べる場合	145
料理長のおすすめ	138
淋病	187

【る】

ルームサービス	141
一般的に尋ねる場合	141
深夜などに尋ねる場合	141

【れ】

礼儀	60
「礼儀を知らない」と言う場合	60
「礼儀正しい」と言う場合	61
「礼儀上…する」という意味の場合	61
劣等感	48

【ろ】

6人座れるテーブル	135
ロングドレス	101

【わ】

私の性質	53
悪気はなかった	66
普通に述べる場合	66
強調して述べるとき	66
悪く思う	69
悪口を言う	64
普通に言う場合	64
強調して述べる場合	64

著者紹介

ボストンアカデミー校長　市橋敬三

　長年の滞米生活によりアメリカ英語を身につける。
　英会話上達の秘訣は「英文法を知っているではなく、使い切れるようにすることにある」と、英会話にとって英文法の不可欠性を、1984年に刊行した著書の中で、日本の英会話教育史上初めて唱えたこの道の草分けであり、現在も第一人者的存在。
　話すための英文法シリーズ4冊(研究社出版)は「英文法イコール英語の長文読解をするためのもの」という長年の誤ったイメージを根底からくつがえし、日本の英会話教育に大きな影響を巻き起こした。
　オハイオ州の名門校のマウントユニオン大学を優等(cum laude)で卒業。
　言語であるアメリカ英語を研究するだけでなく、アメリカ研究学を専攻し、アメリカの歴史、政治、社会、地理、宗教などを研究した後、ニューヨークでビジネス界に身を投じ、これらの体験によりアメリカの真の姿を知悉している数少ない知米家の一人。
　著書に新聞、雑誌の書評欄に掲載され大好評を博し、またAmazon.comで何度も好反響を得た「最新アメリカ英語表現辞典」(大修館書店)など約60冊あり。

アメリカ英語日常会話辞典

2005年2月28日　1刷

著　者──市橋敬三
　　　　　Ⓒ Keizō Ichihashi, 2005
発行者──南雲一範
発行所──株式会社 **南雲堂**
　　　　　東京都新宿区山吹町361 (〒162-0801)
　　　　　電　話 (03) 3268-2384 (営業部)
　　　　　　　　(03) 3268-2387 (編集部)
　　　　　FAX (03) 3260-5425 (営業部)
　　　　　振替口座　00160-0-46863
印刷所／図書印刷株式会社

Printed in Japan　〈検印省略〉
乱丁、落丁本はご面倒ですが小社通販係宛ご送付下さい。
送料小社負担にてお取替えいたします。

ISBN 4-523-31043-2　C0582 〈D-43〉